PASS
Cambridge
BEC 2

An examination preparation course

Ian Wood
Paul Sanderson
Anne Williams

Pass Cambridge BEC 2 Student Book

ISBN 1-902741-08-4

Published by Summertown Publishing Ltd
26 Grove Street
Summertown
Oxford
OX2 7JF
United Kingdom

Produced by the Linguarama Group Pedagogical Unit, 89 High Street, Alton, Hants, GU34 1LG, United Kingdom.

Editor: Anne Williams
Writers: Ian Wood, Paul Sanderson

Series Editor: Elizabeth Clifton

Acknowledgements

Linguarama would like to thank the following companies for their kind permission to reproduce photographs and other copyright material. Linguarama is particularly grateful to the individuals named below for their contribution to the units.

Auto Express: David Johns, Editor • CCH (Case study - The Cash Flow Gap): Copyright 1999 by CCH Incorporated. All Rights Reserved. Reprinted with permission from CCH Business Owner's Toolkit (www.toolkit.cch.com) • Company Digest: Peter Tribe, Editorial Director • Coverdale: The Coverdale Organisation plc is a management and training consultancy based in Leamington Spa, Warwickshire, UK. Since 1965 it has been helping organisations to gain vision, creativity, commitment and skills to bring about sustainable change, performance improvements and enhanced bottom-line results. • The Financial Times • ICI: Geoff Paddock, Senior Group Press Officer • IDA Ireland: Catrina O'Kennedy, Information Manager • Otto Versand (GmbH & Co): Jürgen Bock • Personnel Today: Sarah King, Group Editor • Porters Restaurant: Covent Garden, London • PricewaterhouseCoopers: David Thompson, Senior Manager, Global HR Solutions • Sainsbury's Bank: David Noble, Director of Marketing • Skoda UK: Eilish O'Shea, Public Relations Manager

Every effort has been made to contact the copyright holders who have not been acknowledged and apologies are expressed for any omissions.

Printed in the United Kingdom

Introduction

The Cambridge BEC examination

The **Cambridge Business English Certificate (BEC)** is a new international business English examination which offers a language qualification for learners who use, or will need to use, English for their work. It is available at three levels:

Cambridge BEC 3	Advanced
Cambridge BEC 2	Intermediate/Upper intermediate
Cambridge BEC 1	Lower intermediate.

Cambridge BEC 2 is a practical examination that focuses on English in business-related situations. The major emphasis is on the development of language skills for work: reading, writing, listening and speaking.

Pass Cambridge BEC 2

The book contains:

- **Introduction** An introductory unit which gives you information about the examination and this preparation course. It also gives tips on developing your vocabulary skills.

- **Core units** Ten double units which cover a wide range of business-related topics. Many of the exercise types are the same as those in the examination.

- **Self-study** A section after every double unit to provide consolidation of the vocabulary and functions of the unit. It also contains a focus on a particular grammatical area to enable you to review your grammar systematically.

- **Exam practice** Tests after every double unit to provide further practice in the examination skills you will need.

- **Exam focus** A section in the centre of the book to prepare you directly for the examination.

- **Activity sheets** Pairwork and supplementary activities at the back of the book.

- **Tapescripts** The content of the cassettes.

- **Essential vocabulary** A list of the key vocabulary in each unit.

- **Essential functions** A list of the key functions in the book.

- **Answer key** Answers to **Self-study** and **Exam practice**.

- **Look it up** A reference page to help you find relevant information in *Linguarama English Reference Guide 2*. It also helps you find the English-language websites of the companies mentioned in the book.

Language development in *Pass Cambridge BEC 2*

- **Reading**

  Reading is the most tested skill in the examination. The book therefore contains a lot of reading practice, using authentic, semi-authentic and examination-style texts. Do not panic if you do not understand every word of a text; sometimes you only need to understand the general idea or one particular part. However, you need to read very carefully when answering examination questions; sometimes the most obvious answer on the first reading is not correct and you will change your mind if you read the text again.

- **Writing**

  In the examination you have to write notes, memos, letters and short reports. You are expected to be very concise and pay attention to the task and the word limit. If you have good spoken English, it does not necessarily mean that you can write well. To be successful, you need training and practice.

- **Listening**

  Listening is also a very important skill for the examination and most units contain listening activities. You can find the **Tapescripts** to the cassettes at the back of the book.

- **Speaking**

  You can find help on how to prepare for the Speaking Test in the **Exam focus** section. In addition, there are speaking activities in every unit.

- **Vocabulary**

  Although vocabulary is tested explicitly only in Reading Test Part Four, it is very important throughout the examination. Many exercises in the **Self-study** sections recycle vocabulary from the units. At the back of the book you can find **Essential vocabulary**, which lists the key vocabulary for each unit.

  You will probably meet vocabulary that you do not know in the Reading and Listening Tests, so it is important to have strategies for dealing with difficult words. The **Introduction** unit provides ideas on helping you to guess the meaning of words; it also provides ideas about recording, storing and building your vocabulary.

- **Functions**

  The book reviews and practises functional language such as phrases for arranging an appointment and making requests, suggestions and recommendations. For Cambridge BEC 2 you also need to be able to express such functions in writing. At the back of the book you can find **Essential functions**, which lists both written and spoken forms.

- **Grammar**

  Grammar is systematically reviewed in the **Self-study** sections of the book. However, the review is brief and you may need to supplement the material. To look at a grammar point in more depth, refer to *Linguarama English Reference Guide 2*.

Examination preparation in *Pass Cambridge BEC 2*

- ## Introduction

  The **Introduction** presents the content of the examination and focuses on important examination dates.

- ## Core units and Self-study

  Most units contain at least one examination-style exercise and there are also some examination tasks in **Self-study**. For example, *multiple-choice* and *matching* are both typical examination-style exercises.

- ## Exam practice

  Each double unit is followed by at least two pages of **Exam practice** which supplement the examination practice in the core units and **Self-study**. Complete Listening Tests follow Units 5 and 10. By the end of the book, you will have systematically practised every part of the examination.

- ## Exam focus

  The **Exam focus** section in the centre of the book gives you information about how to succeed in each of the examination tests.

Contents

			Language	Skills

Introduction

Cambridge Business English Certificate 2

Successful Cambridge BEC 2 candidates receive two grades: one for Reading, Writing, Listening and one for the Speaking Test.

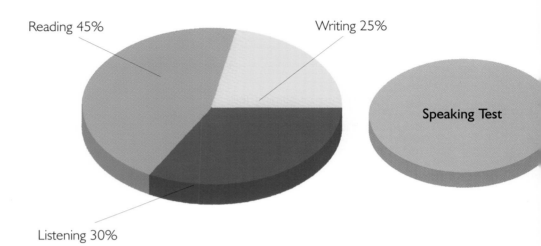

Reading 45%

Writing 25%

Speaking Test

Listening 30%

Single grade (A, B, C, Narrow Fail or Fail)

Separate grade for the Speaking
(1, 2 or No grade)

An overview

The following table gives an overview of the different parts of the examination, how long they take and what they involve.

	Test	Length	Contents
1	Reading & Writing	90 minutes	Reading: 5 parts (45 questions) Writing: 2 parts (memo or note, and formal letter or short report)
2	Listening	40 minutes	3 parts (30 questions) Approx. 12 minutes of listening material played twice
3	Speaking	12 minutes	Interview: 2 examiners and 2 or 3 candidates

Important Cambridge BEC 2 dates

Your teacher will give you some important dates at the start of your course. Write these dates in the boxes below.

Cambridge BEC 2 examination

Your teacher will give you the dates of the written papers but can only give you the date of the Speaking Test after your entry has been confirmed by Cambridge.

- PAPER 1 Reading & Writing Test
- PAPER 2 Listening Test
- Speaking Test (to be confirmed)   Between [   ] and [   ]

Entry date

This is the date by which the exam centre must receive your exam entry.

- Entries must be confirmed by

Grades and certificates

Cambridge sends out results approximately seven weeks after the examination. Successful candidates receive their certificates about four weeks after that.

- Results should be available by

Quiz: Pass Cambridge BEC 2

1 Where would you find the following in this book? Write the unit or page numbers.

1 An expenses claim form
2 Three units which feature internationally famous firms
3 Information for a telephone role-play
4 The tapescript of a presentation about a company's environmental impact
5 A fax writing exercise
6 Advice on how to write reports
7 A **Self-study** exercise on conditionals
8 Functional phrases to use in formal letters
9 A list of websites of companies mentioned in this book
10 A game which requires you to make decisions
11 A list of vocabulary related to marketing
12 Useful tips for the **Cambridge BEC 2** Speaking Test

Understanding new words

During the examination you may have to guess the meaning of new words. There are two main ways to help you understand the meaning of an unfamiliar word.

1 Examine the context around the word.
   - The context may help you understand the meaning of the word.
   - The position of the word in the sentence can help you identify the type of word.

2 Examine the word.
   - Prefixes (e.g. *over-*, *re-*, *multi-*) can give part of the meaning of the word.
   - Suffixes (e.g. *-ly*, *-ship*, *-ment*) can help you decide on the type of word.

1 Look at the prefixes below. What meaning do they give a word?

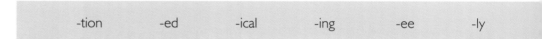

| un- | bi- | sub- | dis- | inter- | pre- |

2 Look at the suffixes below. What type of word does each suffix form?

| -tion | -ed | -ical | -ing | -ee | -ly |

3 Look at the sentences below. Decide what type of word could fill each gap. Then use the context to find a suitable word to complete the sentences.

1 If we _____ our prices any more, we'll start to lose customers.
2 We need to find a suitable _____ for the meeting, big enough for over 100 guests.
3 He spoke _____ so that those at the back of the room could hear him.
4 This is a _____ opportunity to enter the market. I think we could make millions.
5 I'm _____ disappointed with the outcome. It's the worst possible result.
6 She has a lot of experience. _____ , is she the right woman for the job?

Introduction

Using a dictionary

1 Look at the dictionary entry below. Match each letter with the correct information.

in·sur·ance /ɪnˈʃɔːrəns/ **1** n [U] an agreement where you pay money to a company and the company agrees to pay you a sum of money in the case of an accident, illness or damage to your property: *My ~ covers me for loss of earnings. I had to take out ~ when I bought the house.* **2** n [C] ~ **policy** a contract for ~: *The ~ policy runs out next month.*

1 definition   *e*
2 word type
3 compound word
4 spelling
5 pronunciation including word stress
6 grammatical information
7 example sentence with a collocation

2 Work in pairs. Each group of words below has a similar meaning. Discuss the differences between the words. Use a dictionary to help you.

1 A job	**B** occupation	**C** position	**D** profession
2 A site	**B** factory	**C** premises	**D** works
3 A show	**B** reveal	**C** display	**D** appear

Recording and storing vocabulary

1 When you meet new words, you need to record and store them effectively. What are the advantages and disadvantages of storing new words in the following places?

- in your course book in the unit where you meet them
- on a separate sheet of paper
- in a separate vocabulary notebook
- on a computer
- on cards

Where do you store your new vocabulary?

2 Storing new words and phrases on cards allows you to group them, order them, update the cards, test yourself and add new cards at any time. Look at the example below and then make a card for one of the following words.

| industry | manpower | franchise | countersign | economic |

pronunciation

word grammar

a translation

a definition

examples

connected words/opposites

> Negotiate /nəgəʊʃɪeɪt/ (handeln)
> – to discuss in order to come to an agreement
> – verb (regular), ~ + object (a deal, a contract),
>   ~ + prep (with someone, a company)
> – We're negotiating a new supply deal with Arco.
> – I have to negotiate my own pay rises.
> – negotiation, negotiator, (non.) negotiable

3 Some groups of words can be ordered in a logical sequence to make them easier to learn. Put the following into a logical order. Can you add more words to each list?

1 Words describing a supply chain
wholesaler / retailer / end-user / manufacturer

2 Words describing company performance
poor / good / disastrous / encouraging / excellent / satisfactory / unsatisfactory

4 Words which are associated with the same topic can be stored together. Put the following words into the correct group.

| agenda | accountant | business plan | minutes | chairman | negotiate |
| postpone | tax | budget | statistics | AGM | balance sheet |

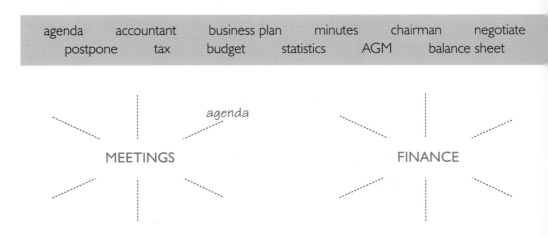

agenda

MEETINGS

FINANCE

Building vocabulary

1 You can use a dictionary to help you build new words using prefixes and suffixes. Complete the table with the correct forms of the missing words.

Verb	Noun	Person	Adjective	Adverb
employ	(un)employment	employer / employee	(un)employed	n/a
globalise	_____	n/a	_____	_____
_____	_____	supplier	n/a	n/a
n/a	_____	n/a	(in)flexible	_____

2 You can use a dictionary to find compound words such as *cost-cutting* and *market share*. Match the following words to form the three different types of compound words below.

Compound nouns

1	staff	order
2	lump	turnover
3	product	sum
4	mail	launch

Compound adjectives

1	user-	productive
2	duty-	wide
3	counter-	friendly
4	world	free

Compound verbs

1	short	hunt
2	under	size
3	head	cut
4	down	list

3 You can build your vocabulary by learning the opposite of words. Write the opposites of the sentences below.

1 They made a *profit* last year.   <u>They made a loss last year.</u>
2 Unemployment has *risen*.   _____
3 This is a *minor* problem.   _____
4 Prices rose *slightly*.   _____

Teamwork

Assessing teams

Speaking ❶ Work in pairs. Look at the following characteristics of a good team. Choose the five most important and put them in order.

What makes a good team?

1 The members work towards a common objective.

2 They discuss roles and allocate them to team members.

3 They co-operate fully with each other.

4 They help individuals develop within the team.

5 The members trust each other.

6 Everyone makes an equal contribution to the team.

7 The members share information effectively within the team.

8 They listen to different points of view.

9 They talk openly and honestly within the team.

10 When people are under pressure, others offer help.

Do you work in a good team? Explain why/why not.

No longer Poles apart

When Peter Welch, President of Cussons Polska and Uroda SA, arrived at Cussons' newly acquired factory in Poland in 1993, he discovered that the concept of teamwork didn't exist. 'The guy who ran it before had a queue of people outside his office waiting for decisions on everything from taking a day's holiday to major investments. All decisions were made by one man.' Cussons entered Poland by taking over a manufacturer of cleaning products in Wroclaw. Two years later they bought Warsaw-based Uroda toiletries. Turnover increased at Wroclaw from £11m to £50m and the smaller Uroda quickly grew into a £22m business. Both businesses are now major brands in Poland and export to other eastern European markets.

1   But in spite of these successes, it is still hard to develop new approaches. 'The company culture here is the result of fifty years of regulation and control,' explains Welch. 'It's not easy to get people to take on responsibility and be accountable when things go wrong. The sales department used to be a guy next to the phone waiting for it to ring.'

2   To help solve these problems, Cussons brought in three expatriate managers to work closely with the local sales staff in project teams. They also brought in senior Coverdale management consultant Keith Edmonds to work on the team's managerial skills and improve communication within the team. Edmonds held two one-week programmes, working on team-building and developing creative thinking.

3   'The imaginative ideas participants came up with were extraordinary - electric.' He describes the programmes as helping people recognise that there is a range of effective management styles. 'We wanted to throw new light on old problems.' The participants responded very positively. In one task, they were given £500 and told to make as much profit with it as possible. 'They came up with amazing ideas,' says Edmonds. 'They put on discos. They went to the Czech border, bought products and then sold them at a profit.'

4   Welch believes the programmes were excellent at 'getting people excited about their jobs'. But he warns, 'we need to ensure that what happens on the programme happens back in the workplace'. The results, however, are already very positive. 'The two programmes cost us about £40,000 in total, including food and accommodation,' says Welch, 'but the returns we are getting from them are huge. We saved about £200,000 from the first programme and we're expecting savings of around £700,000 from the second one.'

The programmes also form the basis of monthly reviews, in which progress is measured against targets set in the programmes. 'You can see the results improving each month. I'm very pleased with the way it has worked out,' says Welch.

ter 50 years of
in a centrally
olled economy,
tern European
panies face the
challenge of
oping effective
ms to improve
efficiency. The
ts, as Cussons
overed, can be
spectacular.

Taken from the Coverdale Review No. 13

❸   Now choose the best title for each numbered paragraph.

Paragraph 1 .....

Paragraph 2 .....

Paragraph 3 .....

Paragraph 4 .....

A   Bringing in consultants
B   Building teams
C   Old attitudes
D   Organising events
E   The benefits of training
F   Thinking creatively
G   Training in the future

Vocabulary ❹ Match the following verbs, prepositions and nouns from the article. Then use the phrases to describe what happened at Cussons in Poland.

1	wait			decisions
2	take		in	ideas
3	bring		for	a consultant
4	work		on	discos
5	come up		with	responsibility
6	put			managerial skills

Speaking ❺ How can teamwork help your class prepare for the Cambridge BEC 2 examination?

Arranging a course

Reading 2 ❶ Carmichael, an American cosmetics group, has a Polish subsidiary. Gina Theismann, Head of Central European Sales, receives a fax from Tom Granger, the local manager in Warsaw. Read the fax and answer the questions.

FROM: CARMICHAEL POLSKA SA   PHONE NO.: 0048222756785   14-JAN-2000   14:43   P01/01

Carmichael, Inc.

Carmichael Polska SA
pl.Starynkiewicza 7/9
02-015 Warsaw
Poland

To: Gina Theismann
From: Tom Granger
Date: 14 January 2000
Pages: 1
Re: Sales team for new product launch in Poland

Hello Gina

Thanks for the profiles of Steve Cerny and Joni Morgan. They both look very good and I think they should work very well together with the three local people here.

I was thinking about getting the whole team together for a week in London. Would the week commencing 9 February be convenient for Steve and Joni?

The team could spend a couple of days on team-building, followed by discussions on the launch. I think we need them to agree on their objectives, roles and schedules by the end of that week. They'll also need to think about communication.

What do you think about the team-building? Should we send them on a survival course? Alternatively, we could bring in a consultant for a more traditional seminar if you think that would be of more use. I've attached a few advertisements from different providers. They are:

• Executive Adventures
• Team Management
• Melville Management Training.

Could you let me know asap about the dates and which provider you prefer?

Regards

1   How many people will be in the sales team?
2   Where and when are they going to meet?
3   What are the objectives of the meeting?
4   When does Tom want an answer?

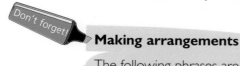

Speaking ❷ Work in pairs. Student A: Look at the Activity sheet on page 145. Student B: Look at the Activity sheet on page 152.

Don't forget!

Making arrangements

The following phrases are useful for making arrangements.

- **Suggesting times and dates**
  How about / What about the following week?
  Shall we say 14 February?

- **Asking for suggestions**
  When would suit you?
  Did you have a time/place in mind?

- **Saying we are unavailable**
  I'm afraid I'm busy then.
  I'm sorry but I can't make it then.

- **Using the present continuous for talking about fixed arrangements**
  They're working on another project until 12 February.

❸ Work in pairs. Look at the advertisements for the team-building courses below. Which of the courses would be the best for the Carmichael team? How would it benefit the five team members and the project?

EXECUTIVE ADVENTURES LTD

Executive Adventures outdoor events help build leading business teams by increasing personal awareness of abilities and complementary skills in colleagues. The events involve a combination of intellectual, physical and practical challenges - meeting and dealing with the unexpected. Our tasks mean that individuals and teams have to:

- identify clear and achievable objectives
- make best use of resources
- work together and communicate openly
- learn to overcome storms and crises.

TEAM MANAGEM

Yes, 2+2 really can = 5! Let the experts at TML show you how. Our team of expert consultants will demonstrate how High Performance Teams really can work. Focusing on issues such as how to form an effective team, team dynamics and communication within teams, our list of specialised seminars includes:
- Self-managing Teams (SMTs)
- Multi-cultural Teams
- Team Leadership
- Fast-forming Teams
- Building World Class Teams

MELVILLE

Management Training

Our unique two-day in-company seminars use board games and simulations to focus on issues such as sales, customer service and team-building. Board games and simulations are fun, time-efficient and allow managers to experience situations without the fear of failure. All games and simulations lead to discussions on management theory and practice. The range includes titles such as:

♦ **Teamwork Challenge** ♦
♦ **Marketing Mania** ♦
♦ **Go for Profit** ♦

Unit 1b

Communication

Keeping in touch

Speaking ❶ Work in pairs. How does your partner use the following forms of communication? Mark them on the graph below.

high

frequency

low

low   high

formality

faxes

letters

e-mails

phone calls

memos

notes

What are the advantages and disadvantages of each form of communication?

Reading ❷ Read the article on the opposite page about using English for international business. Think of a title for each paragraph.

❸ Answer these questions about the article.

1 Why does Ericsson use English as its official language?
2 What can native English speakers do to communicate more effectively?
3 Why are native English speakers unaware of the difficulties of listening to foreign languages?
4 How does Ericsson make its employees more aware of these difficulties?

IS YOUR ENGLISH TOO ENGLISH?

English may be the language of international business but, as Alison Thomas reports, it's not only non-native speakers who need to learn how to use it effectively.

1 Ask a Swedish Ericsson executive 'Talar du Svenska?' and he may well reply 'Yes. But only at home. At work I speak English.' Ericsson is one of a growing number of European companies that use English as their official corporate language. These companies recognise and, at the same time, increase the dominance of English as the language of international communication. Soon the number of speakers of English as a second language will exceed that of native English speakers.

2 Although a company might use English as its official language, its employees are unlikely to be bilingual. Language trainer Jacquie Reid thinks we consistently over-estimate the fluency of non-native speakers. 'We always assume that because their language skills are better than ours, they understand everything we say.'

3 So how should we adapt our use of language and what are the common problems? 'Simplify it,' is Reid's advice. 'Don't over-complicate the message. Reduce what you're saying to manageable chunks.' Reid always tells people to limit themselves to one idea per sentence. 'It's also important to slow down and not raise your voice.'

> *Don't over-complicate the message. Reduce what you're saying to manageable chunks.*

4 Dr Jasmine Patel, a language consultant at Europhone, says different languages also have their own approach to dialogue. 'The British start with idiomatic expressions such as *So, should we get down to it?* and understate important issues with phrases such as *There could be a slight problem.* They also say *That's a good idea, but ...* when they mean *No* and they repeatedly use the word *get* with different meanings. And worst of all, they insist on using humour which is so culture-specific that no-one understands it.'

5 The majority of English native speakers are insensitive to the stress of trying to understand a foreign language in a work environment because they rely on the business world speaking their language. At Ericsson, however, this is not the case. At the UK subsidiary, Ericsson Telecommunications, management training courses include seminars on both language and cross-cultural issues. A frequent comment made in follow-up evaluations is that increased awareness has improved communication and, more importantly, given participants a better understanding of their own language and how others might interpret it. ▣

*Adapted from **Training** Magazine, June 1998*

Speaking ❹ What do you find difficult about understanding native English speakers?

Leaving voice mails

Listening 1 **❶** Frida Andersson, a manager at Sanderlin AB in Stockholm, receives five voice mails. Listen and decide what each speaker is trying to do.

1 .....

2 .....

3 .....

4 .....

5 .....

A	make a complaint
B	request some information
C	change an arrangement
D	decline an offer
E	give feedback
F	confirm arrangements
G	make an offer
H	ask for permission

Which of the calls do you find difficult to understand? Why?

Leaving answering machine messages

When we leave messages, it is important to be very clear.

- **Prepare the listener for the message**
  This is Frank Larsen from Scandinavian Conferences.
  It's 9.30 on Wednesday morning.
  I'm ringing about the sales report.

- **Make requests simple and polite**
  Could you send me the report, please?
  Could you please call me back?

- **Give clear contact information**
  I'm in Helsinki until Friday.
  My telephone number is 346 766.

Speaking **❷** Work in pairs. Look at the tapescript and choose one of the difficult messages. Make it easier to understand.

Taking messages

Listening 2 **1** Frida tries to return two of the calls. Listen and complete the forms below with one or two words or a number.

TICKET ORDER FORM

Event:
Danish Telecommunications
(1)

Name:
Frida Andersson

Company:
Sanderlin AB

Address:
Torhamnsgatan (2)
Stockholm

No. of tickets:
(3)

Date of tickets:
(4)

Other name(s):
(5)

WHILE YOU WERE OUT

To: Sue Mellor

Date: 1 Nov

From: Frida Andersson

Company: Head Office

Tel: ....

Returned your call ☑   Please ring back ☐   Will ring back ☐

MESSAGE

She received (6) _____ .
She's (7) _____ the meeting on 13 November.
She's (8) _____ the following week.
Can you meet her on (9) _____ ?
Could you call her and (10) _____ the date?

Don't forget!

Taking messages

The following phrases are useful for taking messages.

- **Offering help**
  I'm afraid she's not here today. **Can I help you?**
  I'm afraid he's visiting a client. **Can I take a message?**

- **Asking for information**
  Could I ask who's calling, *please?*
  Could you give me *your fax number, please?*

- **Checking information**
  Could you spell that, *please?*
  So, that's *27 November.*

- **Promising action**
  I'll give *her the message as soon as she's back.*
  I'll ask *her to call you as soon as possible.*

Speaking **2** Work in pairs. Student A: Look at the Activity sheet on page 146. Student B: Look at the Activity sheet on page 153.

Self-study 1a

1 Choose the correct word to fill each gap.

> Cussons bought its first Polish **(1)** ..... in 1993. The Canadian company soon discovered that it would take more than a few **(2)** ..... managers to make the business profitable. To improve teamwork, Cussons decided to **(3)** ..... training sessions to improve **(4)** ..... within the cross-cultural teams. Cussons then **(5)** ..... in a management consultant, who **(6)** ..... on managerial and communication skills. Although the programmes cost almost £40,000, the **(7)** ..... over the following twelve months included savings of up to £1m and a clear improvement in management skills and **(8)** ..... towards cross-cultural teams.

	A	B	C
1	branch	subsidiary	office
2	strange	overseas	expatriate
3	allocate	contribute	arrange
4	responsibility	togetherness	co-operation
5	brought	fetched	took
6	developed	worked	put
7	values	benefits	profits
8	attitudes	trust	views

2 Complete the telephone conversation.

- Paul Ricard speaking.
- ▼ Hello Paul. It's Angela. **(1)** __I'm calling about__ the new project. Could we have a meeting for the sales team next week?
- Sure. **(2)** _____ ?
- ▼ Well, **(3)** _____ next Tuesday? Would that be OK for you?
- That should be fine. **(4)** _____ ?
- ▼ I'd like to meet in the morning, early if possible. **(5)** _____ 9.30?
- **(6)** _____ . Could we meet a little later, at say 10.30?
- ▼ Sure, that's no problem. I'll send everyone a memo. Should I ask people to bring anything with them?
- No, just their great ideas.
- ▼ OK, that's fine. See you on Tuesday, Paul.
- Right. Thanks for calling, Angela. I'll see you on Tuesday at 10.30. Bye.

3 Use the words to write sentences with *team*.

She's an effective team member.

multi-cultural

manage   work

successful

develop   organise

effective   (**team**)   leadershi

contribute to   member

improve

courses   building

skills

Present tenses

4 Complete the conversation. Put each verb in bracket: into the correct form of the present simple or present continuous.

- Hi Julie. How are you?
- ▼ Fine, thanks. But I'm very busy at the moment. I **(1** *prepare*) __'m preparing__ for the big meeting tomorrow.
- What's that all about?
- ▼ Oh, it's all about that new product which we **(2** *launch*) _____ next month.
- Yes. I hear it **(3** *not/go*) _____ well.
- ▼ You can say that again. We're behind schedule and I **(4** *begin*) _____ to think we won't be ready in time for the launch.
- What's the problem?
- ▼ The Marketing Department. They're the problem. Every time we **(5** *agree*) _____ on a final design, they **(6** *want*) _____ to make some small change. It's so annoying.
- **(7** *you/meet*) _____ them tomorrow
- ▼ Yes. We're going to tell them we can't make any more changes. We **(8** *not/have*) _____ the time for any more.
- What **(9** *you/think*) _____ they'll say?
- ▼ To be honest, I **(10** *not/care*) _____ . We **(11** *have*) _____ to stick to the schedule. It's as simple as that.

15

Choose the correct word to complete each sentence.

1. OK, I'll (*tell/say*) him you called.
2. Could you give her a (*telephone/call*) after lunch?
3. It's been (*put back/cancelled*) until next week.
4. Unfortunately they are not (*sensible/sensitive*) to other people's difficulties.
5. We're trying to (*rise/raise*) awareness of good telephone practice.
6. Could you (*ask/request*) her to call me back?
7. Please (*adopt/adapt*) your language to the listener.
8. Shall we (*go/get*) down to business?

Put the telephone conversation into the correct order.

Reception

☐ So that's the Alsterhof Hotel for three nights from 22 August. Could you spell the name of the hotel for me, please?

☐ OK, Ms Meier. I'll give Paul the message.

☐ I'm afraid he's in a meeting. Could I take a message?

☐ Thanks for calling. Bye.

☐ And could I ask who's calling, please?

☐ Good afternoon, Pace Systems. Can I help you?

Caller

☐ Sure. That's A-L-S-T-E-R-H-O-F.

☐ Yes, please. I'm ringing about accommodation for his trip to Berlin. I've booked him a room at the Alsterhof Hotel for three nights from 22 August.

☐ That's great. Thanks very much. Bye.

☐ Could I speak to Paul Kerridge, please?

☐ It's Kerstin Meier from Althaus Press in Berlin.

Are the sentences in each pair usually written (W) or spoken (S)? What is the function of each pair?

1. So, that's tomorrow at 10 am in your office.
2. I would like to confirm our meeting tomorrow at 10 am in your office.

3. Would it be possible to postpone the meeting?
4. We couldn't put the meeting back, could we?

5. Please inform me by next week.
6. Let me know by next week, will you?

7. I am afraid I am not available on 12 November.
8. I'm sorry but I can't make it on the 12th.

9. Is it OK if we offer customers a 5% discount?
10. Could we possibly offer a 5% discount?

11. We can take 10% off the price, if you like.
12. We would be willing to reduce the price by 10%.

❹ Complete the sentences with *in, at* or *on*.

1. I'm afraid he's not here _____ the moment.
2. We'll be _____ Copenhagen until Friday.
3. She's busy. She's _____ the phone to someone.
4. The meeting's _____ 3 o'clock tomorrow.
5. I'm afraid I can't make it _____ the 18th.
6. I'm taking two weeks off _____ Christmas.
7. You can call me back _____ 0171 244 666.
8. I'm visiting the Madrid office _____ April.
9. We'll have the meeting _____ the weekend.
10. We should get the report _____ Tuesday morning.

❺ Past simple and present perfect

Add a time phrase to each sentence.

when I started	on Friday so far	lately just
yet	20 years ago	already

so far

1. We haven't bought anything from them this year.
2. You don't need to order them because I've done it.
3. The goods arrived.
4. They haven't phoned the suppliers.
5. I didn't have much experience.
6. We've been very busy.
7. She's gone to lunch but she'll be back in an hour.
8. The company was founded by two brothers.

❻ Complete the telephone message. Put each verb in brackets into the correct form of the past simple or present perfect.

Hi, Stefan. It's Maggie. I (**1** *get*) _____ *got* _____ your e-mail yesterday, but I (**2** *be/not*) _____ able to open the attached report yet. You'll have to tell me which program you (**3** *use*) _____ when you (**4** *do*) _____ it. I (**5** *try*) _____ to open up the document with different programs, but none of them (**6** *work*) _____ so far. I also think we need to discuss one or two things before the meeting. I agree with what you (**7** *say*) _____ in your e-mail about the department training budget being far too small. I (**8** *tell*) _____ Chris that ages ago but he still (**9** *not/do*) _____ anything about it. Anyway, I'd better go. I'll speak to you soon. Bye.

Reading Test Part Four

- Read the text below about interviewing candidates for jobs.
- Choose the correct word from **A**, **B**, **C** or **D** to fill each gap.
- For each gap **I** - **15**, mark **one** letter **A**, **B**, **C** or **D**.

Catching out the dishonest candidate

Most personnel managers agree that job interviews are one of the least objective recruitment methods. But the advantages of testing are not going to change the **(0)** ..... of the interview to employers. The appeal of the interview has everything to do with the **(1)** ..... factor.

Most people believe they are a **(2)** ..... judge of character and trust their instinctive feelings. We might use some kind of test to aid the **(3)** ..... process, but we usually pick a candidate who interviews well, has good **(4)** ..... and an impressive work record.

But **(5)** ..... the candidate lies or is less than completely honest 'This can be a serious, problem for employers', **(6)** ..... Alan Conrad, Chief Executive at Optimus Recruitment. 'The most difficult liars to find are those who **(7)** ..... half-truths rather than complete lies.' Research **(8)** ..... that up to 75 per cent of curriculum vitaes are deliberately inaccurate. The most common practice is **(9)** ..... .

Interviewers should therefore concentrate on areas of **(10)** ..... such as gaps between periods of employment and job **(11)** ..... that seem strange. 'Focusing on these areas will force candidates to tell the truth or become increasingly **(12)** .... This is usually when people signal their **(13)** ..... by their body language. Sweat on the upper lip, false smiles and nervous hand movements all **(14)** ..... discomfort.'

Conrad does not suggest an aggressive police-style interview technique, but insists that **(15)** ..... inspection of a curriculum vitae is absolutely essential. Only by asking the right questions can you confirm the suitability of the candidate or put pressure on those who are being less than completely honest.

Example

0	A attraction	B addiction	C necessity	D temptation

A B C D
■ ☐ ☐ ☐

	A	B	C	D
I	emotion	feeling	human	person
2	reasonable	sensible	substantial	normal
3	choice	selection	identification	discovery
4	examinations	papers	notes	qualifications
5	pretend	think	suppose	fantasise
6	reveals	admits	exaggerates	explains
7	say	tell	inform	talk
8	shows	predicts	calculates	reckons
9	ignorance	forgetfulness	omission	carelessness
10	error	incorrectness	uncertainty	indecision
11	descriptions	advertisements	interpretations	routines
12	untrue	illegal	dishonest	criminal
13	annoyance	anger	anxiety	disappointment
14	indicate	prove	present	picture
15	immediate	tight	near	close

Reading Test Part Five

Section A

- Read the extract from a business management book.
- In most lines **1 - 5** there is **one extra word** which does not fit in. One or two lines, however, are correct.
- If a line is correct, write **CORRECT**.
- If there is an extra word in the line, write the **extra word in CAPITAL LETTERS**.

Example

0 | T | H | E | | | | | |

00 | C | O | R | R | E | C | T | |

Managing Your Business Finances

0   If you want to succeed in the business, you need to know about financial

00   management. No matter how skilled you are at developing a new product,

1   providing with a service, or marketing your wares, the money you earn will

2   slip between your fingers if you do not know how to collect it, keep on track

3   of it, save it and spend or invest it wisely. A poor financial management

4   is one of the main reasons why businesses fail. In many cases, failure

5   could have been avoided against if the owners had applied sound financial

     principles to all their dealings and decisions.

Writing Test Part One (i)

- You are a manager at an auditors called Golding & Co. Your company has just merged with a competitor to become MasonGolding. You have been asked to inform staff of the change of name.

- Write a memo of **30 - 40 words**:

  * informing staff of the new name
  * telling them when to start using the new name
  * asking staff to use only the new name after that time.

Writing Test Part One (ii)

- You are the Human Resources Manager of an insurance company. You want to arrange a 2-day team-building event with Team-Plus for eight sales staff.

- Write a note of **30 - 40 words** to your assistant:

  * telling him to contact the provider
  * saying who and how long the event is for
  * suggesting two possible weekends for the event.

Entertaining a client

Choosing a restaurant

Reading 1 **1** Read the customer satisfaction form. Which three of the criteria are most important for you?

Signet House Restaurants

Thank you for choosing to eat at a Signet House restaurant. We are constantly striving to improve the quality of our service and would welcome your comments. Please help us by taking a few moments to complete this form.

	Excellent	Satisfactory	Poor
Location	❑	❑	❑
Atmosphere	❑	❑	❑
Comfort	❑	❑	❑
Cleanliness	❑	❑	❑
Staff friendliness	❑	❑	❑
Staff attentiveness	❑	❑	❑
Speed of service	❑	❑	❑
Quality of food	❑	❑	❑
Quality of drink	❑	❑	❑
Value for money	❑	❑	❑

We look forward to your next visit.

Signet House, Old School Lane, Worlingham,
Suffolk, NR34 7RZ Tel: 01502 599497

Speaking **2** Work in pairs. Use the criteria above to ask your partner questions about the last restaurant he/she went to.

PORTERS
ENGLISH RESTAURANT

Porters English Restaurant opened in 1979 in the centre of London's Covent Garden with the sole objective of serving quality, exciting English food at very reasonable prices. This concept has proved over the years to be extremely popular with British and international tourists alike.

Over the years **Porters** has continued to evolve gently. We have added air-conditioning, restaurant computer systems and a more modern interior design, which have enhanced both atmosphere and comfort.

Porters has two distinctive areas that are normally available for group dining, with semi-private facilities for around one hundred guests downstairs or up to thirty-five on the upper mezzanine floor.

We have always prided ourselves on our complete flexibility and we will organise every group menu and catering requirement on a totally individual basis. **Porters** is happy to cater for all kinds of different parties: from tour groups with only an hour to spare before going on to the theatre, when speed of service along with the quality of food is of the greatest importance, to more informal and relaxed birthday parties, or even corporate events, wine tastings and company presentations.

So when you're next in Covent Garden, call in and see us.

You won't be disappointed!

Speaking ❹ Would Porters be a suitable restaurant in these situations?

- an end-of-year office party
- an evening with a new client and his/her partner
- a corporate event to launch a new product or service
- a negotiation for a contract with a new client
- an end-of-week meal with a small group of colleagues

❺ Work in pairs. Describe the most memorable restaurant you have ever been to.

Making conversation

Listening 1 **❶** Five people talk about their business trips. Listen and decide which of the questions each speaker answers.

1 .....

2 .....

3 .....

4 .....

5 .....

A	What did you think of the food?
B	How was your journey?
C	What was the factory like?
D	What's your hotel like?
E	How was your journey from the airport?
F	How did the meeting go?
G	How useful was the information we sent?
H	What do you think of Rio?

Listening 2 **❷** Listen to a complete version of the last conversation. How does the first speaker encourage conversation?

Don't forget!

Encouraging conversation

We can encourage conversation in the following ways.

- **Showing interest / surprise**
  Really?
  I'm surprised to hear that.
  Do you?/Did you?/Are you?/Have you?

- **Asking follow-up questions**
  What did you think of ...?
  When are you going to ...?
  How do you feel about ...?

- **Using the speaker's words in a follow-up question**
  ▼ *So the meeting's been postponed until next March.*
  ■ *Next March?*

Speaking **❸** Work in pairs. Develop these statements into conversations. Use the techniques above.

1 The trains were all running late, so I knew I'd miss my flight to Lisbon.
2 And when the bill came, I realised my wallet was in my other jacket.
3 The interview went like a dream and they're going to offer me the job.
4 I love English breakfasts. We have nothing like this in my country.
5 As a way of saying thank you, my boss has given me a few days' holiday.

Speaking ④ Play the game in groups. When you land on a square, talk about the topic. The other students in the group should encourage you to talk further. The game is over when one of the players reaches FINISH.

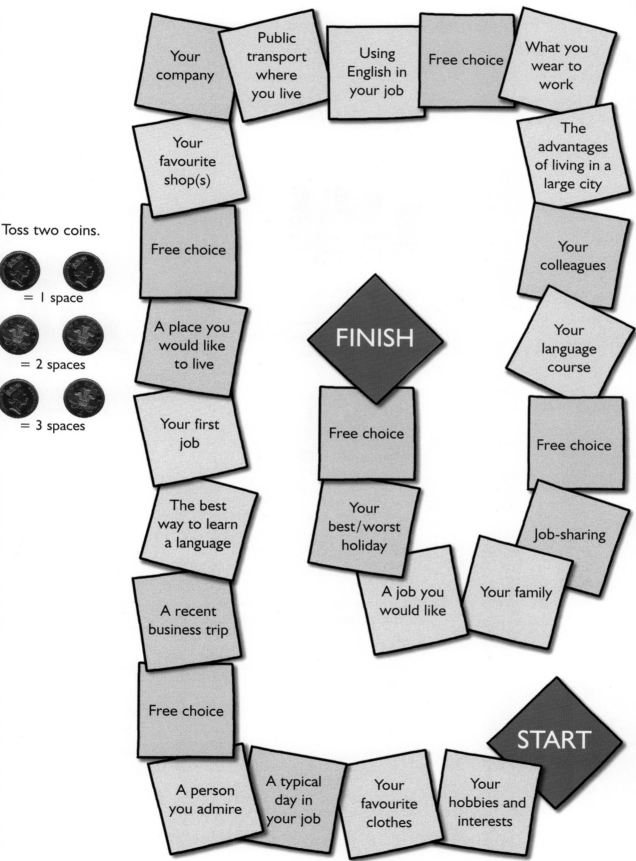

Toss two coins.

= 1 space

= 2 spaces

= 3 spaces

Your company

Public transport where you live

Using English in your job

Free choice

What you wear to work

Your favourite shop(s)

The advantages of living in a large city

Free choice

Your colleagues

A place you would like to live

FINISH

Your language course

Your first job

Free choice

Free choice

The best way to learn a language

Your best/worst holiday

Job-sharing

A recent business trip

A job you would like

Your family

Free choice

START

A person you admire

A typical day in your job

Your favourite clothes

Your hobbies and interests

Corporate hospitality

Mixing business with pleasure

Speaking **1** Read the profiles of the business people below. Choose ways of entertaining them from the following list.

- a meal at an expensive restaurant
- a round of golf
- a sightseeing tour of the city
- an evening at the theatre
- a visit to a sports event
- a shopping trip

A party of **four Japanese businessmen** in their mid-forties. They are on a fact-finding mission to help them decide whether to offer your company a substantial contract.

Andrea Bergen, 38, the Manager of a German computer software company, and her Personal Assistant, **Regina Meier**. Several orders you placed with their company arrived late. As a result, you nearly lost a valued customer.

Pietro Zanelli, 45, the Managing Director of your company's largest client. He is flying in from Rome to finalise one or two small details concerning a major deal with you. His wife, Vittoria, is with him on this trip.

Mike Greenwood, 35, the Sales Manager of Shirts & Shorts, a manufacturer of fashion sportswear. This is a new but important customer. He has a two-day stopover on his way back to New York.

Reading 1 **2** Read the article on the opposite page. Which ways of entertaining business clients are mentioned?

3 Read the article again. Choose the best title for each numbered paragraph.

Paragraph 1 .....

Paragraph 2 .....

Paragraph 3 .....

Paragraph 4 .....

A	Being sociable
B	Building relationships
C	Choosing the right event
D	Choosing the right moment
E	Enjoying corporate events
F	Getting down to business
G	Setting clear objectives

Training to be entertaining and making it pay

Diane Summers picks up some tips on how hosts and clients can mix business and pleasure more effectively.

Got a lunch with a client or contact today? Are you sure your objectives for the meal are clear? If your answer to the last question is yes - having some nice food and getting to know the other person a little better - you could be in need of a training course. Fortunately, one is now available. Called 'Influencing in a Social Context', the three-day programme run by Huthwaite, the UK-based training consultants, will give you the knowledge and skills to plan and achieve business objectives in a social setting while ensuring that your clients and prospects still enjoy themselves.

The first thing the course stresses is that there is no point in taking clients to a rugby match if you are hoping to have some one-to-one conversations. Instead, use a sporting event or the opera, for example, as a 'hook', then arrange a meal afterwards for the more intimate discussions about your company's outstanding record, or whatever business it is that you wish to do.

Another common mistake many businesses make is to send staff to corporate events without telling them why they are there or what they should do. It is not surprising that they see this as a chance simply to stand around having free drinks on the company and chatting to each other rather than talking to clients. Everyone feels uncomfortable in this situation.

Also, many business people seem to be afraid of 3 even mentioning the word 'business' at corporate events. Yet too much social chit-chat and getting-to-know-you-type conversation adds up to missed opportunities. Corporate events need to be seen for what they are - business meetings in a social setting.

A further difficulty lies in deciding exactly when 4 you bring up the matter of business at a social event. Some people simply have poor timing. What client wants to spend an evening at the theatre listening to you whisper half-yearly sales figures into his ear, no matter how exciting you may think they are?

The perfect setting for more relaxed intimate discussions

According to Peter Belsey from Huthwaite, the recipe for success and the key to establishing or building a good business relationship seems to be the ability to mix 'social' conversation with 'purposeful' conversation and to move smoothly and effortlessly between the two. So, if you're having lunch with a client today, ...

*Adapted from the **Financial Times**, 9 March 1998*

4 Using the information in the article, complete each sentence with a phrase from the list.

1 In order to do business without distractions, do not ...

2 At a social event, it is a mistake to ...

3 It is important to choose the right moment to ...

4 The key to establishing a business relationship is to ...

A   tell staff what to do in social settings.
B   combine both business and pleasure.
C   chat to colleagues and ignore clients.
D   improve techniques for social chit-chat.
E   mention the subject of business.
F   take clients to sports events.
G   have a nice meal and a good time.

Speaking **5** What are the advantages and disadvantages of mixing business with pleasure?

Arranging a company visit

Reading 2 **①** Mr Fellini, the Purchasing Manager of Cuore Sportivo, has received this invitation from Angela Goddard of Trackplus Ltd. Read her letter. What is the invitation for?

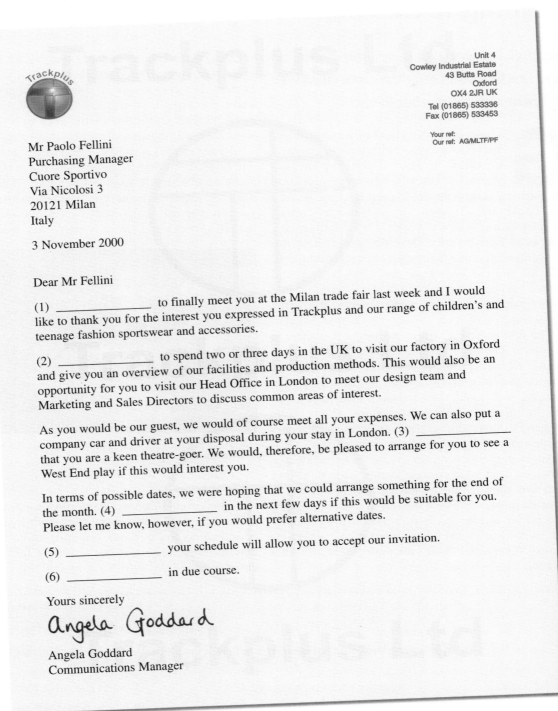

Trackplus

Unit 4
Cowley Industrial Estate
43 Butts Road
Oxford
OX4 2JR UK

Tel (01865) 533336
Fax (01865) 533453

Your ref:
Our ref: AG/MLTF/PF

Mr Paolo Fellini
Purchasing Manager
Cuore Sportivo
Via Nicolosi 3
20121 Milan
Italy

3 November 2000

Dear Mr Fellini

(1) _____ to finally meet you at the Milan trade fair last week and I would like to thank you for the interest you expressed in Trackplus and our range of children's and teenage fashion sportswear and accessories.

(2) _____ to spend two or three days in the UK to visit our factory in Oxford and give you an overview of our facilities and production methods. This would also be an opportunity for you to visit our Head Office in London to meet our design team and Marketing and Sales Directors to discuss common areas of interest.

As you would be our guest, we would of course meet all your expenses. We can also put a company car and driver at your disposal during your stay in London. (3) _____ that you are a keen theatre-goer. We would, therefore, be pleased to arrange for you to see a West End play if this would interest you.

In terms of possible dates, we were hoping that we could arrange something for the end of the month. (4) _____ in the next few days if this would be suitable for you. Please let me know, however, if you would prefer alternative dates.

(5) _____ your schedule will allow you to accept our invitation.

(6) _____ in due course.

Yours sincerely

Angela Goddard

Angela Goddard
Communications Manager

② Read the letter again. Are the following statements true or false?

1 Mr Fellini first met Ms Goddard at the Milan trade fair.
2 Mr Fellini has already seen Trackplus's production processes.
3 Trackplus will pay for Mr Fellini's accommodation expenses only.
4 Ms Goddard would like Mr Fellini to visit at the end of November.
5 Ms Goddard is sure that the dates will be convenient for Mr Fellini.

invitation

❸ Choose the most appropriate phrase (A or B) to fill each numbered space in the letter.

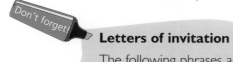

Writing tip:
Always consider your relationship with your reader. This decides how formal or informal your letter should be.

1. A It was really great
   B I was delighted

2. A We'd really like you to come
   B We would like to invite you

3. A I believe you mentioned
   B I'm pretty sure you told me

4. A I would be grateful if you could tell me
   B It'd be nice if you could let me know

5. A I'm really hoping
   B I do hope

6. A I look forward to hearing from you
   B Please drop me a line

Don't forget!

Letters of invitation

The following phrases are useful for formal written invitations.

- **Inviting / Offering**
  We should like to invite you ...
  We should be very pleased if you could ...
  We would be delighted if you could ...

- **Thanking**
  Thank you (very much) for your (kind) invitation to ...
  It was very kind of you to invite me to ...
  I was delighted to receive your invitation to ...

- **Accepting**
  I would be very pleased to ...
  I should be delighted to ...

- **Declining**
  Unfortunately, due to ..., I am unable to ...

Writing **❹ Mr Fellini decides to accept Angela Goddard's invitation. Write a letter of acceptance of 100-120 words:**

- thanking Ms Goddard for her letter
- expressing interest in her suggestions
- accepting the invitation to the theatre
- saying the dates are unsuitable and explaining why
- suggesting an alternative date.

❶ Complete each sentence with a suitable preposition.

1 It's very popular _____ tourists.
2 They pride themselves _____ their flexibility.
3 We organise events _____ an individual basis.
4 We look forward _____ your next visit.
5 You can get good food _____ reasonable prices.
6 The restaurant caters _____ all kinds of parties.
7 When you're next here, call _____ and see us.
8 They offer good value _____ money.
9 The meeting's been postponed _____ Friday.
10 We're a long way _____ a decision.

❷ Re-arrange the words to make questions. Then match each question with a suitable answer.

1 the enjoy meal you did
  Did you enjoy the meal?   B

2 the how meeting go did
  _____

3 's like your what hotel
  _____

4 was the how restaurant
  _____

5 was like flight what your
  _____

6 problems us have finding did you any
  _____

7 journey you a have good did
  _____

8 of think you place did what the
  _____

9 you here when get did
  _____

A Wonderful. And it had a great atmosphere.
B It was absolutely delicious, thank you.
C Not at all. I just followed your instructions.
D Just a few minutes ago. Sorry I'm late.
E Very comfortable, thanks.
F Not bad, I suppose. We did make some progress.
G I didn't really get a chance to look round.
H Fine, thanks. There were no delays this time.
I Fine, thanks. It only took a couple of hours.

❸ Complete each sentence with the correct form of the word in capital letters.

1 SATISFY
  Customer _____ is high.

2 LOCATE
  The restaurant is _____ in the centre of London.

3 COMFORT
  The seats are extremely _____ .

4 CLEAN
  Restaurant _____ and speed of service are important criteria.

5 ENTERTAIN
  Perhaps we should organise some
  _____ for our visitors.

Auxiliary verbs

❹ Write a follow-up question to each of the statements below. Use only words from the boxes.

Is	Do
Are	Does
Was	Did
Have	Could

n't

I?
you?
he? she? it?
we?
they?

1 The meal was pretty awful, actually.   Was it?
2 He doesn't speak much French.   Doesn't he?
3 When the bill came, I realised I'd lost my wallet.
4 I much prefer continental breakfasts.
5 They couldn't remember the name of their hotel.
6 We've postponed our end-of-year party.
7 They aren't going to offer him the job.
8 She's taking them to an English restaurant.

❺ Complete each question with a question tag.

1 It was a lovely meal, _____ ?
2 It's a good place to take a new client, _____
3 Their trip's been postponed till June, _____
4 You don't work for ICI, _____ ?
5 You haven't met Mr Roberts, _____ ?
6 The meeting went well, _____ ?
7 You won't forget to get there early, _____ ?
8 There's a mistake here, _____ ?

Read this letter. Replace the numbered expressions with more suitable phrases.

Dear Mr Rausch

(1) **It was fantastic** to finally meet you in Berlin last month and I would like to thank you for the interest you expressed in our products.
(2) **We really want you to come** to spend two or three days in the UK to visit our factory to get an overview of our facilities and production methods.
(3) **It'd be nice** if you could tell me in the next few days if the end of March would be convenient for you. Please let me know, however, if you have alternative dates.
(4) **I'm really hoping** your schedule will allow you to accept our invitation.
(5) **Please drop me a line** in due course.

Yours sincerely

Complete the sentences with the following words.

missed	golden	social
poor	free	valued

1 Staff sometimes see this as a chance to have _____ drinks on the company.

2 Corporate events are an opportunity to do business in a _____ setting.

3 The _____ rule of corporate hospitality is to turn every social event to business advantage.

4 Unfortunately, some people have _____ timing.

5 It's a _____ opportunity if you don't mention business at a corporate event.

6 We always look after _____ customers.

Complete each sentence with a suitable preposition.

1 We would like to give you an overview _____ our production facilities.

2 You can bring the matter _____ at the meeting.

3 They placed a car _____ my disposal.

4 There is no point _____ taking a client to a rugby match if you want a serious discussion.

5 The key _____ a good business relationship is mixing purposeful and social conversation.

4 Match the words to make phrases.

1	a round of	mission
2	a fact-finding	golf
3	a trade	tour
4	a sightseeing	event
5	a shopping	fair
6	a sports	trip

5 Complete the sentences with the following verbs.

place	meet	set
finalise	build	

1 It was generous of them to _____ my expenses.

2 We can _____ details at the meeting next week.

3 We hope he'll _____ an order with us.

4 Corporate events are a good chance to _____ relationships with new customers.

5 It helps if you _____ clear objectives for staff who are attending a corporate event.

Countability

6 Choose the correct word to complete each sentence.

1 He set up several (*business/businesses*) in the UK.

2 Gianna gave me some good (*advice/advices*) about how to do business in Italy.

3 There (*is/are*) still some work to be completed.

4 I need some (*information/informations*) about marketing opportunities in Sweden.

5 The news about the contract (*is/are*) good.

6 Have you made (*much/many*) progress?

7 I've only got (*a few/a little*) money, I'm afraid.

8 We've spoken (*much/many*) times on the phone.

9 I asked if I could help with her (*luggages/luggage*).

10 He has a lot of (*experience/experiences*) of dealing with Japanese business people.

11 We rely a great deal on her (*knowledge/knowledges*) of market opportunities.

12 I have (*little/a little*) time at the moment, so we could talk about it now.

Reading Test Part Two

- Read the letter below about a late delivery of goods.
- Choose the correct sentence from **A - I** to fill each gap.
- For each gap **I - 5**, mark **one** letter **A - I**.
- Do not use any letter more than once.

Dear Mr Walker

I am writing in response to your letter of 13 May concerning the late delivery of order no. S19/611.

First of all, I would like to apologise for your order not being delivered on the date we agreed in our contract and also for the difficulties you have had in trying to reach me. **(0)** ....✓ The dispute involved all employees and, as a result, all production came to a complete standstill. Secretarial and administrative staff were also involved; this is why it has been so difficult for you to reach me.

I am pleased to inform you that the dispute has now been settled and we should be back to normal production within a few days. **(1)** .... I have spoken to our Production Manager this morning, and he informs me that it will take at least ten days to clear these.

I can assure you that we are doing everything we can to reduce this delay. To help us achieve this, our production workers have agreed to work overtime. Our overseas sales outlets are also returning stock to help us fulfil these outstanding orders. **(2)** .... We do realise, however, that the goods may not arrive in time for you to meet your commitments to your own customers.

You mentioned in your letter that any losses suffered due to late delivery would result in your taking legal action against us. I would like to point out, however, that our contract does state quite clearly that in the event of unforeseen circumstances, we cannot be held liable if we are unable to meet agreed delivery dates. **(3)** .... However, we do realise that the delay in delivering your order puts you in a very unfortunate position with a new customer. In view of this, we are prepared to allow you to cancel your contract with us so that you can place your order with another company. **(4)** .... We have been in touch with our legal advisers on this matter, and they have informed us that we are not legally responsible for any claims you might bring against us.

We deeply regret the inconvenience this delay has caused you and other established customers. **(5)** .... I would like to take this opportunity to assure you that we will continue to do so in the future.

I would be grateful if you could telephone or fax me to let me know how we should proceed with your order.

I look forward to hearing from you.

Yours sincerely

P. Davies
Manager

Example

0 A B C D E F G H **I**

A   I think you must agree that an industrial dispute is something over which we have no control.

B   Yours is only one of many other important orders that have been delayed by this dispute.

C   Perhaps we could discuss alternative dates which would be suitable to you.

D   We must make it clear, however, that we will not accept any responsibility in the event of legal action.

E   I am sure you will agree that until this incident we have provided a reliable and efficient service.

F   Other customers of ours have been very understanding of the difficulties we have been experiencing.

G   Nevertheless, as you can imagine, we are now faced with a sizeable backlog of orders.

H   We are giving your own order priority and we hope to deliver by the end of next week.

I   As you may have heard in the news, we have experienced a major industrial dispute.

Reading Test Part One

- Look at the four job advertisements and the sentences below.
- Which job does each sentence **1 - 7** refer to?
- For each sentence, mark **one** letter **A**, **B**, **C** or **D**.
- You will need to use some of the letters more than once.

A   **Marketing Secretary**

We are seeking a brilliantly organised and mature department secretary to act as PA to the Head of Marketing and provide administrative support to three other busy department heads. The successful applicant must have strong secretarial skills and knowledge of up-to-date information technology. A good sense of humour and excellent communications skills are essential.

B   **Science Marketing Assistant**

This position would suit a recent science graduate with an interest in developing a career in marketing in a publishing environment. Marketing experience is preferable but not essential as full training will be given. The company also has a strong internal recruitment policy.

C   **Assistant Museum Manager**

Reporting directly to the Manager, your role will be to help improve visitor services. The flexible 35-hour week will regularly involve working weekends and evenings. Previous experience of working in a similar role is required. This is initially a one-year appointment but may be extended.

D   **International Management Consultant**

Suitable bilingual applicants will have worked in a similar position here or abroad for at least two years. Excellent communication and presentation skills are vital, as is the willingness to invest the necessary time in order to succeed in a highly competitive and challenging market.

Example

0   A knowledge of languages is important for this job.

A B C **D**
▭ ▭ ▭ ▬

1   A knowledge of computer skills would help you get this job.

2   This company likes to promote people from within the firm.

3   The successful applicant must be prepared to work long hours in this job.

4   Previous experience is not necessary for this job.

5   In this job, the official working hours will change from week to week.

6   In this job, you would have to report to more than one person.

7   This job would be unsuitable if you were looking for long-term employment.

Ordering goods

Placing an order

Speaking ❶ Otto, the Hamburg-based mail order company, has suppliers all over the world. What qualities do you think Otto looks for in its suppliers?

Reading 1 ❷ Korinna Krämer works at Otto's headquarters. She wants to order some goods from Italian suppliers. Read her fax to Otto's Italian subsidiary. Are the statements below true or false?

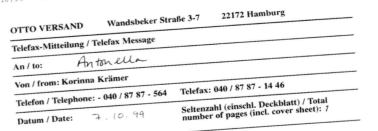

```
07/10/99   12:44:09   +0049 040 / 64 61 - 14 46   KORINNA KRAEMER   PAGE 1
```

OTTO VERSAND	Wandsbeker Straße 3-7	22172 Hamburg

Telefax-Mitteilung / Telefax Message

An / to: Antonella

Von / from: Korinna Krämer

Telefon / Telephone: - 040 / 87 87 - 564   Telefax: 040 / 87 87 - 14 46

Datum / Date: 7. 10. 99   Seltenzahl (einschl. Deckblatt) / Total number of pages (incl. cover sheet): 1

Dear Antonella

Mr Hubner and the other buyers have finalised their reports and recommendations for the summer collection. Mr Hubner thinks that there might be problems with the different lengths of some of the skirts included in the catalogue.

As a result, we've decided to buy the following items in a standard length only.

Supplier	Item	Article no.
Cristi	Skirt	315227
Faci	Skirt	314739

This, of course, means cancelling other lengths of the skirts this year.

We'd also like to reduce the order quantity. Would it be possible to order only 400 pieces of each article? Please let me know asap.

Best regards

Korinna

1 The products mentioned in the fax are men's clothing.
2 The buyers have now decided what they want to include in the summer catalogue.
3 Mr Hubner wants to order the skirts in different lengths.
4 Korinna wants to increase the order quantity by 400 pieces.
5 She asks Antonella to reply quickly.

3 Read Antonella's reply to Korinna and answer the following questions.

1 What is the purpose of Antonella's fax?
2 Why was she surprised by Korinna's fax?
3 What is Antonella going to do?

THE OTTO VERSAND COMBINED GROUP

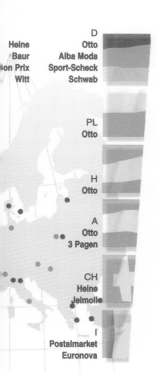

8/10/99   10:26:19   +39 70 300 689   ANTONELLA ZANETTI   PAGE 1

OTTO ITALIA

Via Toscana, 1 - 20068 S. BOVIO DI PESCHIERA BORROMEO (MI) -
Tel. 02-75.393.1 - Fax TXT 02-70.300.689 / HW 70.300.713

FROM:	ANTONELLA ZANETTI	**DATE:**	8 10 99
TO:	KORINNA KRAEMER		
FAX:	02 7 0 300 889		
RE:	CRISTI & FACI SKIRTS	**PAGE:**	1 OF 1

Dear Korinna

Thanks for your fax concerning the Cristi and Faci skirts for the summer katalogue articles 315227 and 314739 respectively. I discussed the problems regarding the two skirts with Mr Hubner during his trip to Italy. The skirt made by Faci has a slit at the bottom which might make it difficult if the customer wanted to change the lenght of the skirt so we agreed the vendor would have to supply the skirt in two different lenghts. Mr Hubner thought it might be better to leave the two different lenghts of the Cristi skirt. The skirt has a special knitting technik and it might be difficult if the customer wanted to shorten it. When Mr Hubner left Italy I thought we had sorted the problems out. I was surprised by your fax cancelling the other sizes. Please let me know if you definitly want to cancel the other lenght skirts. As for reducing the total quantity, I will wait for confirmation of the information about lengths before I contact the vendors. Thanks and best regards.

Antonella

4 How could you improve Antonella's fax? Make notes under the following headings.

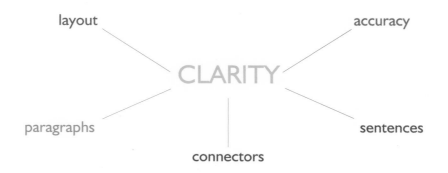

layout

accuracy

CLARITY

paragraphs

sentences

connectors

5 Now write a clearer version of Antonella's fax.

Listening ❶ Korinna receives Antonella's reply and phones her. Listen to their conversation. What does Antonella have to do?

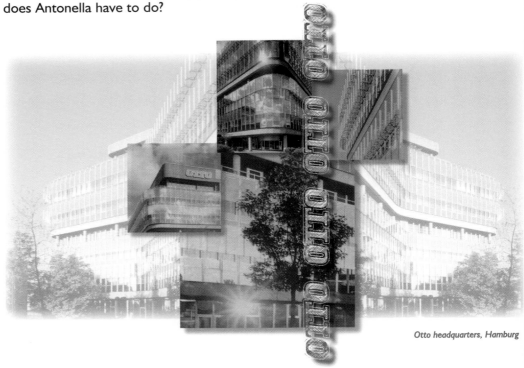

Otto headquarters, Hamburg

❷ Listen again. What phrases are used to express the following functions?

1 Stating the reason for calling	I'm ringing about ...
2 Confirming information	
3 Requesting action	
4 Promising action	
5 Thanking	
6 Referring to future contact	

How would these functions be expressed in a formal letter?

Functions ❸ Match each function with two of the phrases: one from a telephone conversation and one from a letter.

1 Referring to a letter
2 Suggesting
3 Giving information
4 Asking for confirmation
5 Asking for information
6 Reminding

Why don't we ...?
I got your letter about ...
I would be very grateful if you could send me ...
Further to your letter of ...
I trust you will find the following points of interest.
We propose ...
May I remind you that ...?
Let me know when you have a definite date.
Here's the information you wanted.
Can you send me details on ...?
Don't forget that ...
Could you please confirm the date?

Confirming changes

❶ Antonella speaks to the vendors and then faxes Korinna. In each numbered line of her fax there is one wrong word. Find and correct each mistake.

```
8/10/99      13:10:24        +39 70 300 689       ANTONELLA ZANETTI       PAGE 1
```

OTTO ITALIA
Via Toscana. 1 - 20068 S. BOVIO DI PESCHIERA BORROMEO (MI) -
Tel. 02-75.393.1 - Fax TXT 02-70.300.689 / HW 70.300.713

FROM: ANTONELLA ZANETTI   **DATE:** 8 10 99
TO: KORINNA KRAEMER
FAX: 02 7 0 300 889
RE: SKIRT RANGE   **PAGE:** 1 OF 1

Dear Korinna

1   Further to our phone conversation on this morning, both Cristi and Faci have
2   confirmed so they will produce articles 315227 (Cristi) and 314739 (Faci) in
3   standard length only. They are also able to reduce these quantity to only 400
4   pieces for each skirt. Please advice whether the measurements charts we
5   already have will need changed or not. Does this mean all knitted skirts will
    now be produced in a standard length?

Thanks and best regards.

Antonella

❷ Write a 30-40 word reply to Antonella:

- telling her not to change the charts
- confirming that all knitted skirts will be in a standard length
- suggesting a delivery date for the finished order.

Cash flow

Managing cash flow

Speaking **1** What are typical inflows and outflows for your company?

Reading **2** Read the case study on the opposite page about a computer business owned by Steve and Sue Quick. Answer the following questions.

   1 How much money does Steve receive when he takes the order?
   2 How much does the system cost to build and install?
   3 When does he receive final payment?

Now summarise Quick Computers' problem.

3 Do these words refer to inflows or outflows in the Quick Computers case study?

> down payment   total sales price   early settlement discount
> labour costs   wages   outstanding balance   to finance   interest

4 Complete the bar chart with information from the Quick Computers case study.

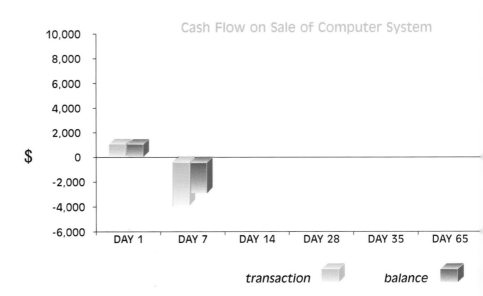

Cash Flow on Sale of Computer System

transaction   balance

Case Study

The cash flow gap

Steve and Sue Quick own Quick Computers, a small computer company in Atlanta. The company builds and installs office computer systems and employs two people.

Background

When a customer places an order, Steve charges 10 per cent of the total sales price as down payment. The customer is then billed for the remainder after the system has been installed. The total sales price of a small office computer network is $10,000. The components are priced at $4,000 and come from one supplier. This supplier offers a 2 per cent discount if Steve pays for the supplies no later than 10 days after receiving them. Steve always takes advantage of early settlement discounts.

The problem

On day 1 Steve receives the $1,000 down payment and orders the parts. He pays for these on day 7 ($4,000 less 2 per cent early settlement discount = $3,920).

The system is ready for installation by day 28 and Steve calculates direct labour costs of $2,700. As he pays his employees every two weeks, these wages are paid on days 14 ($1,200) and 28 ($1,500). A week later, on day 35, the system is installed, with further labour costs of $300. The customer is then billed and given credit terms of 30 days. Finally, on day 65, Steve receives the outstanding balance of $9,000.

The cash flow gap opens on day 7 when Steve pays for the supplies; it widens to $5,920 by day 35. This means he has to finance, and possibly pay interest on, the $5,920 for 30 days until the customer pays the final $9,000.

> **'The more we sell, the less cash we have.'** Steve Quick

Adapted from **CCH Business Owner's Toolkit**

Speaking **5** Work in pairs. Think of three other reasons why many small companies fail.

Improving cash flow

Writing **1** Steve and Sue are finding it difficult to pay suppliers because of a shortage of cash. Steve e-mails Barbara Capel, a friend and management consultant, to ask for help. Read the e-mail. What solution are Steve and Sue considering?

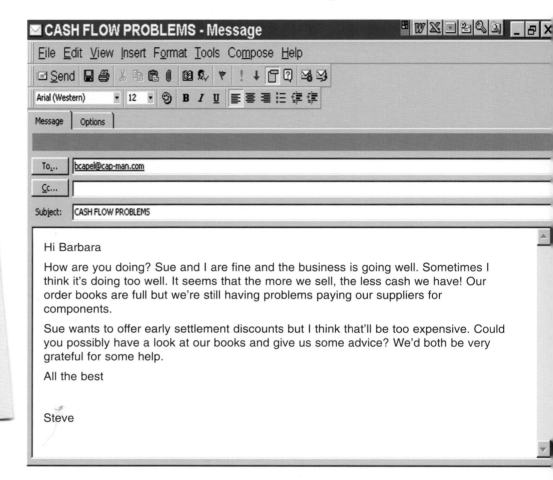

Writing tip:
E-mail is becoming increasingly important in the business world. Although e-mails are often short and informal, their style always depends on the writer's relationship with the reader.

CASH FLOW PROBLEMS - Message

File   Edit   View   Insert   Format   Tools   Compose   Help

Send

Arial (Western)   12   B *I* U

Message   Options

To... | bcapel@cap-man.com
Cc... |
Subject: | CASH FLOW PROBLEMS

Hi Barbara

How are you doing? Sue and I are fine and the business is going well. Sometimes I think it's doing too well. It seems that the more we sell, the less cash we have! Our order books are full but we're still having problems paying our suppliers for components.

Sue wants to offer early settlement discounts but I think that'll be too expensive. Could you possibly have a look at our books and give us some advice? We'd both be very grateful for some help.

All the best

Steve

2 Write a 30-40 word reply to Steve:

- agreeing to help
- commenting on Sue's idea
- suggesting a time and place to meet.

Listening **3** Barbara discusses the cash flow problem with Steve and Sue. Listen to their discussion. What are their attitudes to early settlement discounts?

4 Listen again and answer the following questions.

1   How does Barbara describe the problem?
2   How many customers would be interested in a 1% early settlement discount?
3   Why doesn't Steve want to offer discounts?
4   What is the company's average monthly turnover?
5   What does Steve forget to include in his calculations?
6   How much extra would the 1% discount really cost the company?
7   How would a 2% discount improve Steve's cash flow?
8   What action do Steve and Sue decide to take?

5 Look at these possible uses of conditional forms. Write them in the appropriate groups below.

- to describe actions/situations we do not expect to happen
- to describe hypothetical actions/situations
- to describe actions/situations we expect to happen
- to respond to suggestions we do not agree with
- to make indirect suggestions

If + present simple,	*will* *going to* + infinitive *might*	If + past simple,	*would* *could* + infinitive *might*
			to describe actions/situations we do not expect to happen

Now look at the tapescript and underline all the examples of conditional forms. Find examples which match three of the uses above.

Speaking **6** Work in pairs. Look at these suggestions for improving Quick Computers' cash flow. Choose the best five ideas. How would they benefit the company?

- ask customers for cash on delivery
- reduce credit terms from 30 to 20 days
- add penalty charges for late payment
- pay suppliers after 30 days, not 10
- reduce inventory to a minimum
- find cheaper suppliers
- pay staff monthly
- cut the staff wage bill
- increase prices
- increase sales

❶ Re-arrange the words to make formal phrases from written correspondence.

1 interest trust I find you the points following of will

   <u>I trust you will find the following points of interest.</u>

2 the you could please confirm date

   _____

3 you remind may that I

   _____

4 of further letter your to

   _____

5 you very I would grateful be could if

   _____

6 you concerning fax your for thank

   _____

❷ You are a buyer at a mail order company. You have decided to reduce the size of next year's catalogue. This means cancelling part of an order.

Write a letter of **100 - 120** words to the supplier:

* informing the supplier
* explaining the cancellation
* saying which articles you wish to cancel
* apologising for the cancellation
* confirming the delivery date for the order.

❸ Complete the puzzle. Which word runs vertically through the answers?

1 p	i	e	c	e	s	

1 We'd like to order 400 ....., please.
2 The ..... of the workmanship is excellent.
3 They're too long. We'll have to ..... them.
4 We'll ..... the order if they put their prices up.
5 Otto is Europe's largest ..... company.
6 The ..... can supply the goods you want.
7 If it's too short, change the ..... .
8 I'd like to ..... the quantity from 300 to 200.
9 Our chief ..... does all the negotiating with suppliers.

❹ Complete each sentence with the correct form of the word in capital letters.

1 RECOMMEND
   The _____ retail price is £24 a unit.

2 FINAL
   We'll _____ the order details by the
   end of next week.

3 DELIVER
   Can I arrange _____ on 6 May?

4 MEASURE
   I think we'll have to change the _____
   for the new catalogue.

5 SUPPLY
   We deal with a number of Italian _____

6 STANDARD
   We've decided to _____ the lengths
   of all the skirts in the summer catalogue.

Intentions and arrangements

❺ Complete each conversation with *will*, *going to* or the present continuous.

1 ● Could you send me the measurements?
   ▼ Sure, I (*fax*) ____'ll fax____ them to you
      now.

2 ● When (*you/leave*) _____ ?
   ▼ In about an hour or so. I (*order*) _____
      a taxi in a few minutes.

3 ● What (*you/do*) _____ this weekend
   ▼ Nothing special. After such a stressful week, I
      (*relax*) _____ .

4 ● Can you make the meeting on 16 June?
   ▼ I'm afraid I can't. I (*visit*) _____
      suppliers then.

5 ● Two pages of the fax you sent are missing.
   ▼ Oh, sorry about that. I (*fax*) _____
      them through again.

6 ● So what have you decided? Where
      (*you/take*) _____ Mr Ifem when he
      comes next week?
   ▼ We usually take clients to Hunters - but maybe I
      (*try*) _____ somewhere new.

Use the words to write sentences with *cash*.

We are experiencing a cash flow gap.

pay   delivery

on

gap   flow

discount   (**cash**)   price

forecast   payment

in

shortage   situation

Complete each sentence with a suitable preposition.

in	at	for	of
on	as	within	

1 Our cash flow problems meant paying financing costs in the form of interest _____ a loan.

2 We can't pay _____ our supplies.

3 Is there a discount if we pay _____ cash?

4 We've priced the work _____ $3,000.

5 They offer a discount if we pay _____ 10 days.

6 The bill includes the cost _____ labour.

7 We always ask for 10% _____ down payment.

Complete the text with the following phrases.

cash on delivery	30 days net
down payment	early settlement discount
outstanding balance	penalty charges

We offer our customers a range of credit terms. Normally, when we sell a product we ask for a **(1)** _____ of 10% of the total sales price. The **(2)** _____ is then due when the customer takes delivery of the finished product. We normally offer **(3)** _____ with an **(4)** _____ of 1% if the customer pays within the first 10 days. For customers that pay late we add **(5)** _____ . If they regularly pay late, then we insist on **(6)** _____ .

---

4 Which of the four words in each group cannot combine with the word in capital letters?

1 CASH
flow   purchase   terms   discount

2 PAY
wages   costs   interest   supplies

3 PAYMENT
down   late   labour   cash

4 COSTS
labour   customer   production   financing

Conditionals 1 and 2

5 Complete the conversations with the following words.

might	don't
'd	were
increase	wouldn't
will	did
would	insisted on
'll	look

1 ● How do you feel about offering discounts?
   ▼ We have no choice. If we _____ , we _____ never solve our cash flow problems.

2 ● I suppose the best way is to make our customers pay on delivery.
   ▼ Are you crazy? If we _____ cash on delivery, we _____ have no customers within 3 months!

3 ● We should be able to find a cheaper supplier.
   ▼ Yes, that's true. We _____ be able to find one if we _____ hard enough.

4 ● We'll just have to increase sales, that's all.
   ▼ That won't help. If sales _____ even more, our cash flow problems _____ get worse.

5 ● Why don't we pay our staff monthly?
   ▼ I was thinking about that idea. But the staff _____ be too happy if we _____ it.

6 ● Maybe we'll have to cut staff wages.
   ▼ I don't think that's a very good idea. How _____ you feel if your wages _____ cut?

Reading Test Part Two

- Read the article below about the use of hold music on company telephones.
- Choose the correct sentence from **A - I** to fill each gap.
- For each gap **I - 5**, mark **one** letter **A - I**.
- Do not use any letter more than once.

Putting the caller on hold, not the business

Have you ever wondered just how many potential customers call your company every day, fail to get through and hang up never to try again? Most businesses still take it for granted that callers will wait patiently for a connection and see no reason to do anything more than tell them what they already know - that the lines are busy. **(0)** ..... If it is something familiar and easy to listen to, potential customers are far more likely to wait or try again later.

In the USA, 70 per cent of calls are put on hold and the average business person spends up to 60 hours a year waiting to speak to people on the phone. Despite these facts, businesses show an amazing lack of imagination when it comes to the simple task of keeping potential customers happy while they wait. **(1)** ..... Anyone who has listened to such a statement repeated over and over again understands why callers hang up.

A recent study in the USA found that 60 per cent of on-hold callers hang up, and over 30 per cent do not try to call again. It also shows that callers find voice messages aggressive and cheap, leaving the caller with a negative picture of the company. **(2)** ..... Furthermore, if it is well-chosen and enjoyable, it can help shape a customer's image of the company. This is already established practice in the retail sector, where music is used to encourage shoppers to spend more time in the store. Research also shows that playing accordion music in a supermarket, for instance, can increase sales of French wine.

In the USA, however, some companies have developed the idea further, offering more than just music to callers. This fast growing part of the on-hold business is referred to as on-hold marketing: the combination of music and brief promotional messages. **(3)** ..... Others are putting on-hold time to equally good use with airlines announcing special offers and hotels taking the opportunity to describe conference facilities.

One company says that its on-hold marketing programme, combining messages with 'brand enhancing' music, reduces hang-ups by 50 per cent and increases sales by up to 20 per cent. **(4)** ..... For maximum effect the music should communicate a message in line with the company's image. According to the usual stereotypes, classical music says 'quality and intelligence' while pop music says 'youth and fun'.

On-hold International, a Florida-based marketing company, says a typical 4-minute piece of on-hold marketing comprises 15-second segments of music alternating with 15-second voice messages. During the voice messages the music fades into the background. **(5)** ..... Donald Rich, the company's founder says that messages that leave the caller both informed and entertained work better than those that deliver just the hard sell. 'It should not be used as an obvious selling tool. It should be more of a relaxing experience for the customer, a you-mean-a-lot-to-us type thing.'

Example

0 A B C D E F G H **I**

A   Cable television companies, for example, are already using it to advertise forthcoming movies.

B   The research included experiments to see what kind of music makes people more likely to hold on.

C   Most companies still only offer these callers a brief voice message saying they are on hold.

D   An experiment using such music in a canteen led to an annoyed employee switching it off.

E   The switch from one to the other helps keep potential customers interested.

F   Music, on the other hand, is easier to listen to and far more relaxing.

G   The music that works best is the easy-going kind that causes activity in this part of the brain.

H   Such claims demonstrate the importance of choosing the right on-hold music.

I   However, businesses that want to increase sales can do so by providing on-hold callers with music.

Reading Test Part Five

Section A

- Read the extract from a business management book.
- In most lines **1 - 5** there is **one extra word** which does not fit in. One or two lines, however, are correct.
- If a line is correct, write **CORRECT**.
- If there is an extra word in the line, write the **extra word in CAPITAL LETTERS**.

Example

0 | C | O | R | R | E | C | T | | |

00 | T | H | R | O | U | G | H | | |

0	Many organisations are seeking to take advantage of flatter management
00	structures by moving through to self-managed teams. In our experience, these
1	teams produce very impressive results. However, as the companies
2	we work with can tell it you, they are neither a 'soft option' nor a 'quick fix'.
3	Self-managed teams operate in dramatically different ways from the other
4	teams and they can only succeed if the organisational culture, along with a
5	number of systems and procedures, are been re-shaped. Thus, changing to
	self-managed teams requires top level support.

Section B

- Read the job advertisement below.
- In each line **1 - 5**, there is **one wrong word**.
- For each line **1 - 5**, write the **correct word in CAPITAL LETTERS**.

Example

0 | I | N | V | I | T | I | N | G | |

00 | D | I | R | E | C | T | L | Y | |

0	The company is invited internal applications for the position of Financial
00	Controller at our Helsinki office. Reporting direct to the Commercial Director,
1	you will be supported by a small team and responsible to all accounting
2	functions of the company. Like a young team leader, you will have experience
3	of implementing as well as develop systems and controls. You will also have
4	that ability to communicate effectively with all levels of management and be
5	expect to provide advice to non-financial staff at all levels. Experience of
	project costing would be an advantage.

Brand power

Selling points

Speaking ❶ Work in pairs. Look at the products below. What brand of each product would your partner buy? Why?

Listening 1 ❷ Five people explain why they bought one of the products. Listen and decide the main reason for each purchase.

1 .....

2 .....

3 .....

4 .....

5 .....

A	after-sales service
B	environmental-friendliness
C	performance
D	price
E	reliability
F	reputation
G	style
H	user-friendliness

Reading 1 **❶** Read the newspaper article about large supermarket chains in the UK. How are they stretching their brands into new markets?

Banking on a brand

As supermarkets continue to diversify into new markets, Madhur Ranatunga asks whether there is anything that supermarkets are not prepared to sell.

Is a quiet revolution under way in the nation's shopping habits? Are we gradually allowing an increasingly select number of large companies to take care of all our basic requirements? The supermarket chains certainly hope so. 'People don't have the time to shop around any more. If they're happy with the quality of a company's service, then they're likely to buy other product types from them as well,' says Jim Austin, an industry analyst.

With the major supermarket brands such as Tesco, J Sainsbury and Asda already offering financial services, credit cards, own-label clothing, mobile phones, and cut-price electrical goods including computers, Austin firmly believes that the supermarkets' diversification is set to continue.

'The UK retail food market is saturated, so their only real prospect of growth is either to enter foreign markets or diversify into new markets at home.' Tesco and J Sainsbury have done both. Having already bought foreign subsidiaries, both large supermarket chains have set up their own banks in order to offer customers financial services such as personal loans, mortgages and savings accounts.

Together, the two new banks took over £2bn of customer deposits within the first year of trading. 'They are winning business by using a lower cost base to offer their customers better interest rates on savings than traditional banks,' says Austin.

However, there are question marks over long-term profitability. The traditional providers say there is bound to come a point when the new banks will eventually want to widen margins and boost profits. 'When they start to raise prices, they might create bad publicity, which could hurt their brand,' says one observer. 'How will a major supermarket react, for instance, when it is faced with having to repossess a regular shopper's home?'

Shoppers, however, do not share these fears. A recent survey of 1,000 people by brand consultants Cook & Pearson concludes that shoppers will continue to buy a wider range of goods and services from supermarkets. Many people said that they would be prepared to buy a supermarket own-label car or even a house from a supermarket-branded estate agent. Interest was also shown in combining a food shopping trip with a visit to a supermarket dentist.

Loyalty schemes are another incentive for customers. 'Most supermarkets now offer bonus points with every purchase. These points add up to free air miles or cash discounts, so it really pays to stay loyal to the brand in all its diversified forms,' says Austin.

❷ Read the article again and answer the questions.

1 Why are the large UK supermarket chains diversifying?
2 How are the supermarkets able to attract business in the banking sector?
3 What are the risks involved with brandstretching?
4 How do the large supermarket chains encourage brand loyalty?

Speaking **❸** Imagine your local supermarket offered its own brand of the products and services mentioned in the article. Would you buy them? Why/Why not?

Up to 15% discount off package holidays with 12 Reward vouchers

Half price UK hotel breaks for only 2 Reward vouchers

Just 2 Reward vouchers for 2 free UCI cinema admissions
(all UCI excluding Leicester Square)

Fly free to Paris from London for only 12 Reward vouchers (Plus Tax)

Sainsbury's Bank

Reading 2 **1** Look at the extracts from advertising leaflets for Sainsbury's Bank. Match them with the financial products in the box.

> A home insurance
> B mortgage
> C personal loan
> D savings account
> E VISA credit card

1 **E**njoy an Extra Large
20% introductory no-claims
discount STARTING TODAY

2 **M**oney available WITHIN DAYS

3 **W**elcomed at over 14 million outlets
AROUND THE WORLD

4 **T**he fixed rate
way to PEACE OF MIND

5 **W**here else will you find
INSTANT ACCESS to your money
and NO FEES?

6 **P**lus additional Reward Points
WHEREVER you use it

7 **F**lexible cover,
competitively priced

SAINSBURY'S BANK FRESH BANKING™ FROM SAINSBURY'

Speaking **2** What would be the advantages and disadvantages of buying all of these financial products from the same provider?

Listening 2 ❸ David Noble, Director of Marketing at Sainsbury's Bank, talks about the marketing of Sainsbury's financial services. Listen and answer the questions.

1 Who is the target customer?
2 What marketing methods does Sainsbury's Bank use?
3 How has Sainsbury's Bank attracted customers?
4 What advantages has Sainsbury's Bank over traditional banks?
5 Why does David Noble think it is safe to stretch the Sainsbury's brand?
6 How has the Sainsbury's brand developed?

David Noble, Director of Marketing at Sainsbury's Bank

Listening 3 ❹ Listen to the interview again. This time, the cassette will pause at certain points. Choose the best phrase from the list below to continue the conversation.

brand damage	major retail group	financial services
competitive advantage	bad publicity	value for money
direct mail	poor customer service	high overheads
over 700,000 customers	public relations	Sainsbury's brand

Speaking ❺ Use some of the phrases in the box to give a brief summary of David Noble's interview.

Public relations

What is public relations?

Listening 1 **1** Eilish O'Shea, Public Relations Manager at Skoda UK, talks about her job. Before you listen, decide whether the following are the responsibility of the PR or Marketing Department at Skoda.

- communication with the press
- research into the public's needs
- development of the company's reputation
- brand development
- decisions about product pricing
- public awareness of company values

Now listen and check your answers.

Volkswagen Group

Eilish O'Shea, Public Relations Manager, Skoda UK

2 Match the verbs with the phrases to describe the role of the PR Department at Skoda. Then listen to Eilish again and check your answers.

1	manage	the press, television and radio
2	deal with	the public relations strategy
3	provide	long-term relationships
4	give	goodwill and understanding
5	maintain	an accurate picture of the company
6	build	the press and public with information

Describing duties and responsibilities

The following phrases are useful for talking about responsibilities.

My job is to ...
I'm responsible for ...
My job involves ...
In this job you have to ...

Work in pairs. Find out about your partner's duties and responsibilities.

The benefits of good PR

Listening 2 **1** Eilish explains how Skoda changed public attitudes to the brand when it was re-launched in the UK in 1995. Before you listen, suggest how the company achieved this. Then listen and check your answers.

*Taken from **Auto Express**, June 1998*

2 Listen again and choose one letter for the correct answer.

1 People used to make jokes about Skoda because they thought
   A the look of the cars was strange.
   B the quality of the cars was poor.
   C the cars were very boring.

2 Central European engineering
   A had very high standards traditionally.
   B only started to improve after 1948.
   C did not develop during the communist era.

3 Skoda re-launched its brand in 1995 with
   A a range of new models.
   B a new network of showrooms.
   C a major advertising campaign.

4 Good press is more powerful than advertising because
   A it communicates the message more quickly.
   B the message can reach a lot more people.
   C it is based on independent opinion.

5 The company took journalists to the Czech Republic
   A to show them the quality of the production plants.
   B to enable them to attend the launch of the Octavia.
   C to thank them for the positive press they gave Skoda.

6 According to a recent UK consumer survey,
   A the company has sold over 40,000 cars in the UK.
   B Skoda drivers are the most satisfied car owners.
   C central European engineering is the best in Europe.

7 Eilish thinks the success of PR is best measured by
   A customer satisfaction surveys.
   B the amount of press coverage.
   C the company's turnover.

8 The most satisfying part of Eilish's job is
   A working in a small team.
   B having responsibility and influence.
   C solving difficult problems.

Speaking **3** **Work in pairs. What is the public image of your partner's company and its products/services? Does your partner share the same view of the company?**

The Skoda Octavia production plant at Mlada Boleslav, Czech Republic

Organising a PR event

Reading **1** **Eilish organised the UK press launch of the Skoda Octavia in 1998. Complete her launch schedule on the opposite page with the tasks below.**

A Ensure all equipment, branding displays and paperwork etc. are transported to venue.
B Be available to answer questions on all aspects of products/brands.
C Send out invitations and monitor replies.
D Send guests confirmed details of venue, dates, times and format.
E Choose and book venue.
F Ensure all guests have access to information/personnel/products.
G Begin writing press information and designing information packs.

Volkswagen Group

UK Press Launch of Skoda Octavia

Advance preparation

3-4 months ahead
- Set UK 'on sale' date.
- Make sure launch date does not clash with other manufacturers.
- (1) .....
- Decide on best event format for launch.
- Decide on invitation list (target most important motoring magazines, national papers, major regional papers and freelance journalists).

6 weeks ahead
- (2) .....
- Organise photographer for launch.
- (3) .....
- Send requests for attendance at launch to senior executives.

3 weeks ahead
- Send details of event to venue.
- Vehicles arrive for preparation and running in.
- Photography takes place. Choose pictures for press information packs and send to printers.
- (4) .....

1 week ahead
- Finalise details with venue (room bookings, presentations, menus, parking etc.).
- Prepare welcome information and itineraries for guests.
- Final brief for Skoda staff, venue, vehicle management staff.
- (5) .....

At the event
- Ensure everything runs smoothly.
- (6) .....
- (7) .....
- Enjoy yourself.

Speaking **2** Work in pairs. Your company is launching a new product in four months' time. Agree on the following details. Then present your ideas to the class.

- the name of the product
- the venue for the launch
- the date and time of the event
- some details of the event programme
- a final date for returning replies

Writing **3** Write a formal letter inviting a journalist to the launch. Write 100-120 words. Include the five points above.

1 Read through the unit. Find words which can go before or after *brand*.

.......to stretch........   ....power.......

....

         (a) brand   ....

....

....

2 Complete the text with the correct form of the following verbs.

diversify	enter	break into	grow
saturate	target	set up	boost

When we first **(1)** _____ the market fifteen years ago, it was **(2)** _____ fast. We **(3)** _____ a local production facility, which kept our costs down and **(4)** _____ our profits considerably. But cut-price imports started to come in and it wasn't long before the market was pretty much **(5)** _____ . That's when we realised we had to **(6)** _____ and **(7)** _____ new markets. So, we developed a range of leisurewear and after a lot of hard work we managed to **(8)** _____ that market just six months later. Progress has been slow but it's certainly been worthwhile.

3 Complete the table.

Verb	Noun	Adjective
....	commitment	....
diversify	....	....
....	....	saturated
....	attraction	....
....	....	reliable
....	strength	....
encourage	....	....
....	....	growing

4 Complete each sentence with a suitable preposition.

1 I've always been very happy _____ their service.

2 They're diversifying _____ all sorts of new markets.

3 We set _____ our bank in January 1998.

4 The company was faced _____ a saturated market.

5 It pays to stay loyal _____ the brand.

6 The vouchers can be exchanged _____ air miles.

7 We're competing _____ other supermarkets.

8 We're committed _____ customer service.

5 Match the words. Then read through the unit to check your answers.

1	financial	advantage
2	loyalty	services
3	supermarket	clothing
4	competitive	scheme
5	own-label	chain

Futures

6 Choose the correct future forms to complete the conversation. In some cases both forms are appropriate.

● Sven, how are the preparations going for the new product launch?

▼ They're going OK. (*We'll / We're going to*) launch the new product with a TV campaign in about three weeks.

● A TV campaign? (*That'll / That's going to*) cost a lot of money.

▼ Well, we think it's such an important product that (*we'll / we're going to*) spend half our advertising budget on it.

● Half the budget? What else (*will you / are you going to*) do?

▼ Well, (*we'll / we're going to*) use a lot of point-of-sale advertising and do a mailshot next month.

● (*Will it / Is it going to*) target only existing customers?

▼ At first, yes. But if the TV ads go well, then (*we'll / we're going to*) do a larger follow-up mailshot. (*We'll / We're going to*) have to see what happens.

7 Re-arrange the words to make predictions.

1 customers to are buy more likely products

_____

2 diversification the continue to set is future in

_____

3 there be problems some to bound are

_____

4 I 'll no soon it happen doubt 've

_____

Choose the correct word to fill each gap.

The role of the PR department

The primary role of public relations is to talk to the press and the public in order to (1) ..... accurate information from the heart of the company. The overall (2) ..... is to provide information about the company's brands and its (3) ..... so that the public has a positive (4) ..... of the organisation. An essential part of this process is (5) ..... good long-term relationships with the press. Marketing, on the other hand, is more to do with (6) ..... customers' needs and developing the right products to (7) ..... those needs at an affordable price. Marketing (8) ..... the public through advertising, whereas public relations works more with the press and broadcast media.

1	A display	B communicate	C explain
2	A objective	B responsibility	C duty
3	A reputation	B goodwill	C values
4	A look	B image	C aspect
5	A staying	B maintaining	C remaining
6	A viewing	B deciding	C identifying
7	A satisfy	B provide	C manage
8	A touches	B reaches	C gets

Match the phrases to make sentences. Then order them to describe a product launch schedule.

A	Prepare information packs and send	the replies.
B	Ensure all guests have	them to the printers.
C	Send invitations and monitor	the details.
D	Shortly before the launch, brief	access to the products.
E	Choose and book	the venue.
F	Check everything and finalise	all staff involved.

Which word in each group is the odd one out?

1	reputation	brand	image	opinion
2	attitude	awareness	product	understanding
3	PR	campaign	marketing	advertising
4	facility	plant	factory	company
5	invitation	programme	schedule	itinerary
6	manufacture	display	build	produce

4 Complete each sentence with the correct form of the word in capital letters.

1 RESPONSIBLE
Working in a small team means a lot of personal _____ , which I enjoy.

2 AWARE
We're trying to raise public _____ of the brand in Europe.

3 DEPEND
The power of the press is that it is a journalist's _____ opinion.

4 AVAILABLE
We'll release details regarding _____ of the product next week.

5 REPUTE
It's available from all _____ dealers from 16 May.

6 SATISFY
Fortunately, nobody is _____ with our new product.

7 ADVERTISE
We've placed _____ in newspapers.

8 COVER
The new model was given a lot of _____ in the national motoring press.

Articles

5 Complete the text by adding *the*, *a* or *an* where necessary. Some gaps will remain empty.

The Octavia production plant

Shortly before (1) ..... official UK launch of the Octavia, 100 journalists were invited on (2) ..... organised tour of (3) ..... production facility at Mlada Boleslav in (4) ..... Czech Republic. The factory was opened in 1996 and is one of (5) ..... most advanced in the world. At the plant, (6) ..... independent component suppliers also have production facilities, manned by their own staff, producing (7) ..... doors, seatbelts etc. All (8) ..... other suppliers are linked to the production control system and (9) ..... deliveries of parts and materials are made 'just-in-time' to (10) ..... precise schedule.

Reading Test Part One

- Look at the export market reports about four central European countries.
- Which country does each sentence 1 - 7 refer to?
- For each sentence, mark **one** letter **A**, **B**, **C** or **D**.
- You will need to use some of the letters more than once.

A | This was the first central European economy to emerge from recession and start growing stronger. Continued growth in the gross national product of five per cent or more is likely over the next few years. The privatisation of former state industries continues and major projects are being developed, notably in the power generation industry.

B | Although the gross national product has been rising marginally since 1994, the country is still facing economic difficulties, most notably a large trade deficit. Despite these problems, its currency has remained stable against those of its major European trading partners. Privatisation is well advanced, with 75 per cent of wealth now created by the private sector.

C | Despite the government's privatisation programme, industrial production is still dominated by large state-owned manufacturing enterprises. However, smaller private companies are starting to emerge, particularly in the service sector. The country is placing a high priority on rebuilding and modernising its infrastructure and a wide range of products and services are actively being sought.

D | The country's transformation into a market economy has been slow and difficult. However, with its strategic position, substantial natural resources and skilled and multi-lingual workforce, it is likely to become a major European industrial and trading power. Export success in this market requires careful research, patience and a lengthy commitment.

Example

0 The location of this country could well have an impact on its future.

A B C **D**

1 The majority of business in this country is privately-owned.

2 This is the fastest growing economy of the four countries.

3 This would be a good market for construction companies to enter.

4 In order to succeed in this country, you need to plan for the long term.

5 In this country there is very little privately-owned industry.

6 A lot of money is being invested in this country's energy sector.

7 This country imports a lot more than it exports.

Reading Test Part Four

- Read the article from a trade magazine about office computer networks.
- Choose the correct word **A**, **B**, **C** or **D** to fill each gap.
- For each gap **1 - 15**, mark **one** letter **A**, **B**, **C** or **D**.

Making computers work for you

It is a typical day at the office - a senior manager is away when an urgent letter arrives from one of her clients. Meanwhile someone has (**0**) ..... that the wrong price list has been sent out and half of the last (**1**) ..... has been returned because the addresses are out of date. After a lot of time and effort has been (**2**) ..... sorting out all these problems, someone asks (**3**) ..... the new computer system didn't (**4**) ..... all of this from happening. Unfortunately, such problems are (**5**) ..... .

One firm which used to have serious computer problems is Brinkman Lewis, a professional services firm. David Callaghan, a partner at the firm, (**6**) ..... : 'The initial problem for us was that we had all this information on computers around the office but didn't know what to (**7**) ..... with it.'

Finally, Brinkman Lewis decided to (**8**) ..... a network linking all the machines in the office. (**9**) ..... than simply asking one of the senior managers to (**10**) ..... responsibility for information technology, the firm brought in (**11**) ..... Zoe Edlington to plan the development of its network. She began by upgrading the (**12**) ..... telephone system so it could be integrated with the computers to provide closer links between the (**13**) ..... of the firm. She then began finding other ways in which the information already on the network could be (**14**) ..... more effectively.

The strategy worked. The company soon realised that there could be a market for such a (**15**) ..... , and before long Zoe Edlington was head of the firm's new network consultancy business.

Example

0	**A** discovered	**B** recognised	**C** detected	**D** revealed

A ▬ **B** ☐ **C** ☐ **D** ☐

1	**A** campaign	**B** postage	**C** mailshot	**D** launch
2	**A** spent	**B** lost	**C** taken	**D** employed
3	**A** where	**B** what	**C** when	**D** why
4	**A** avoid	**B** prevent	**C** block	**D** frustrate
5	**A** common	**B** average	**C** traditional	**D** general
6	**A** convinces	**B** discusses	**C** refers	**D** explains
7	**A** make	**B** try	**C** have	**D** do
8	**A** manufacture	**B** found	**C** introduce	**D** make
9	**A** Rather	**B** Other	**C** Instead	**D** Opposite
10	**A** confirm	**B** manage	**C** exercise	**D** accept
11	**A** agent	**B** specialist	**C** master	**D** authority
12	**A** former	**B** once	**C** existing	**D** ongoing
13	**A** members	**B** colleagues	**C** workmates	**D** subscribers
14	**A** used	**B** worked	**C** practised	**D** operated
15	**A** result	**B** clarification	**C** solution	**D** decision

Relocation

Why do companies relocate?

Speaking ❶ Work in pairs. Discuss the following questions.

- Why do companies relocate to another part of the same country?
- Why do they relocate to another country?

Reading 1 ❷ Read the extract from a brochure about relocating to Ireland. Choose the best title for each paragraph.

Paragraph 1 .....

Paragraph 2 .....

Paragraph 3 .....

Paragraph 4 .....

Paragraph 5 .....

Paragraph 6 .....

A	Good quality of life
B	Attractive running costs
C	Pro-business environment
D	Financial aid
E	State-of-the-art telecommunications
F	Sophisticated transport logistics

IDA IRELAND
INDUSTRIAL DEVELOPMENT AGENCY

Thinking of relocating?
Six reasons why you can't beat Ireland

1 Ireland enjoys some of the lowest employment costs, one of the lowest rates of inflation and one of the lowest telecommunications tariffs in Europe. These all add up to lower overheads and greater savings.

2 Generous grants are available towards set-up costs. This includes capital investment, training and employment costs, as well as grants towards investment in R & D projects.

3 Successive governments have recognised the importance of providing appropriate infrastructures and fostering an environment that is supportive of industry. Legislators and regulatory authorities work closely with companies to ensure that start-up and expansion plans run smoothly.

4 Ireland has invested more than US$5 billion in recent years to give it one of the most sophisticated telephone networks in Europe.

5 With exports accounting for 80% of national output, it is not surprising that Ireland has a highly efficient distribution network, which brings most of Europe within 24 - 48 hours by truck. In addition, frequent scheduled flights from international airports located throughout the country provide direct access to other European countries and the United States.

6 Ireland's cities are becoming increasingly cosmopolitan yet unspoiled countryside and some of the most spectacular scenery

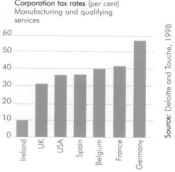

Corporation tax rates (per cent)
Manufacturing and qualifying services

Source: Deloitte and Touche, 1998

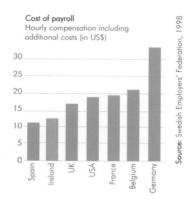

Cost of payroll
Hourly compensation including additional costs (in US$)

Source: Swedish Employers' Federation, 1998

in Europe are always nearby. Residents enjoy ready access to a range of leisure activities, more varied than ever before, from theatres and restaurants to golf, horse-riding and fishing.

It is not surprising that over the last two decades, more than 1,100 overseas companies have relocated to Ireland and are now trading successfully worldwide!

Adapted from Achieve European competitive advantage in Ireland, published by the IDA

Grammar ❸ Underline five adjectives in the text. What are their comparative and superlative forms?

Speaking ❹ Put the six reasons for relocating to Ireland in order of importance for your company.

Arranging to relocate

Speaking   **1**   Work in pairs. Discuss the following questions.

- Why do people relocate to another country?
- What arrangements do people have to make when relocating?

Reading 2   **2**   Fenway Software is relocating several employees to Dublin. Read this report about a relocation company, Executive Relocation Services (ERS). Tick (✓) the services it offers in the table on the opposite page. Cross (✗) any services ERS does not offer.

Date: 12 November 2000

Report on: Suitability of Executive Relocation Services (ERS)

Introduction
This report aims to assess whether ERS meets Fenway's needs (see attached document) in relocating employees and families to Dublin, Ireland.

Findings
ERS offers a comprehensive house search service including Internet pre-viewing. Although it offers no partner employment service, ERS does place children in local schools. ERS also arranges all necessary documentation and offers full packing, storage and shipping services. ERS's costs compare favourably with competitors.

Conclusion
It was concluded that ERS would fulfil most of our key needs.

Recommendations
ERS was felt to offer a high quality service. However, it is proposed that no final decision should be made until other companies have also been considered.

Amanda Ramone
Human Resources Manager

Fenway Software, Inc.   □ 26 Cork Road   □ DUBLIN 1   □ Tel: +353 1 668 5509   □ Fax +353 1 668 5510

Fenway's needs	ERS	Worldwide Relocation
Accommodation search	✓	
Visas and work permits		
Removal and shipping assistance		
School search		
Integration programmes		
Partner employment assistance		

Don't forget!

3 Complete the information below with phrases from the ERS report.

Report writing

The following phrases are useful when writing reports.

- **Introduction**
  The aim/purpose of this report is to ...
  This report sets out to ...
  _____

- **Conclusion**
  It was decided/agreed/felt that ...
  No conclusions were reached regarding ...
  _____

- **Recommendations**
  We would recommend that ...
  It is suggested that ...
  _____

Listening **4** Bob Richards phones Amanda Ramone to discuss another relocation company, Worldwide Relocation. Listen and complete the table at the top of the page.

Vocabulary **5** Look at the tapescript. Underline any words and phrases which refer to similarity or difference.

Writing **6** Which relocation company should Fenway choose? Write a report comparing the two companies and making your recommendation. Write 100-120 words.

Writing tip:
ts should be
y laid out to
them easy to
They often
de headings such

ntroduction
Conclusion(s)
Recommendation(s).

New premises

Getting information

Listening 1 ❶ Gerald Slater works for PLP Immobilier, an international property consultancy in Paris. He gives a client directions to an office site. Listen and mark the correct office on the map below.

2 Jim Flowers telephones Gerald Slater to ask for some information about the office site. Listen and complete his notes.

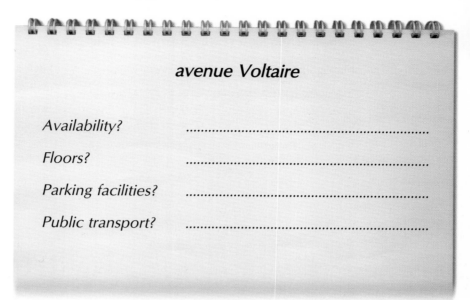

avenue Voltaire

Availability? ....

Floors? ....

Parking facilities? ....

Public transport? ....

3 Listen again and complete the information below.

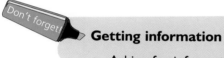

Getting information

- **Asking for information**
  We can ask for information using a fixed phrase followed by a noun.
  I'd like to know about availability.

  _____

  _____

- **Checking information**
  We can use the following phrases for checking information.
  Sorry, I didn't get that. Could you say that again?

  _____

Speaking **4** Work in pairs. Student A: Look at the Activity sheet on page 145. Student B: Look at the Activity sheet on page 152.

5 Work in pairs. Discuss what is important when choosing a new office site. Consider location, price, amenities and any other points which you think are important.

Leasing office space

Speaking ❶ Work in groups. Jim Flowers decides to lease the avenue Voltaire property. Look at the floor plan below. Which rooms do you think the company should allocate to the following? You must reach agreement in your group.

Management	Staff	Facilities
Managing Director	Sales (*12*)	Boardroom
Sales Manager	Accounts (*4*)	Reception area
Chief Accountant	Clerical staff (*8*)	Photocopier room
Shipping Manager		Post room
		Kitchen
		Staff smoking room
		Stores/Stationery

Suggesting

The following phrases are useful when we make suggestions.

Let's ...
Why don't we ...?
How/what about ...?
I think we should ...
Perhaps we could ...
Couldn't we ...?
If we ..., we could/should ...

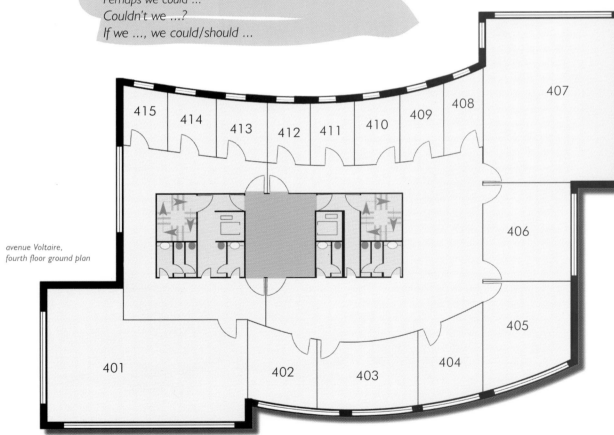

avenue Voltaire,
fourth floor ground plan

Notes

- The smaller offices (408-415) have movable partitioning between them.
- The larger offices (401-407) can be partitioned to make them smaller.
- All doors can be moved and repositioned. Extra doors can be added.

You are interested in renting another property in Paris from the same agent as Jim. Read the information below and your colleague's handwritten notes. Write a letter of 100-120 words to PLP asking for further information.

- Which companies share the site?
- Which underground stations are nearby?
- How many floors are there in the building?
- Additional car-parking? Where?
- We only want 1 floor. Possible?

IMMOBILIER

▸ **Property details**
32 rue de la Paix

▸ **Agents**
PLP Immobilier
Tel 00 331 43 98 95 56

▸ **Type of property**
Office

▸ **Tenure**
Leasehold

▸ **Condition**
New

Location

▸ 32 rue de la Paix is prominently located in a well-established and fast-growing corporate business area. The site is shared with an impressive selection of companies and organisations. There is easy access to public transport from 32 rue de la Paix with numerous bus routes which service the area. Two metro stations are also within walking distance. In the immediate locality there is a wide range of bars and restaurants as well as most major high street shops. Facilities in the area are therefore excellent.

Description

▸ 32 rue de la Paix is an impressive, high-quality multi-storey office building and is ideally suited for a modern tenant's needs. It offers a mixture of open plan and single offices on typical rectangular floors of approximately 410 sq.m with excellent natural light. Underground car parking for 60 cars is provided, and additional surface car parking is available nearby by separate arrangement.

Accommodation

	SQ. M.	SQ. FT.
Seventh floor	426.9	4,595
Sixth floor	412.7	4,442
Fifth floor	408.8	4,400

Full amenities

▸ 8 passenger and goods lifts
▸ Air conditioning
▸ Underground car parking
▸ Natural light on three sides
▸ Prestigious reception
▸ Quality finishes throughout
▸ Toilets on each floor
▸ Standby generator

Viewing

▸ Strictly by appointment only

The details given in respect of this property are believed to be correct. However, their accuracy cannot be guaranteed and they are expressly excluded from any contract.

Self-study 5a

❶ Complete the paragraph with the following words.

investment	savings	costs
tariffs	grants	overhead	rates

Ireland enjoys very low employment (1) _____, one of the lowest (2) _____ of inflation and one of the cheapest (3) _____ for telecommunications in Europe. These all add up to lower (4) _____ and greater (5) _____ . In addition, generous (6) _____ towards set-up costs are available, as is financial help towards (7) _____ in R & D projects.

❷ Complete the report below with the correct form of the following verbs.

offer	make	assess
consider	conclude	fulfil
recommend	arrange	compare

Introduction
The aim of this report is to (1) _____ whether Fast Track UK would be a suitable company to use in relocating employees and families to York.

Findings
Fast Track UK (2) _____ a comprehensive house search service and a full packing and transport service. Fast Track UK also (3) _____ all necessary documentation.

Conclusion
We can (4) _____ that Fast Track UK (5) _____ most of our key needs. Their costs (6) _____ favourably with competitors.

Recommendations
However, we (7) _____ that no final decision (8) _____ until other relocation companies (9) _____ .

❸ Complete the words to make reasons for relocating to Ireland.

1   Ireland offers people a g_ood_ qual_ity_ of li_fe_ .

2   Ireland has a hig_____ effici_____ distribution netw_____ .

3   Ireland offers compa_____ financial incen_____ to se__ up busi_____ there.

4   Ireland has a highly sophis_____ telephone net_____ .

5   The cos_____ of runn_____ a comp_____ are very attra_____ .

❹ Think of two companies that you know. Complete the sentences to compare the companies.

1   Both _companies are based in the USA._
2   Neither company _____
3   Unlike _____
4   _____ whereas _____
5   Like _____
6   In terms of _____ , _____ is better.

Comparatives and superlatives

❺ Correct the mistakes in the sentences below.

1   Job opportunities are ~~more~~ greater than in many other European countries.

2   The range of leisure activities is now varieder than ever before.

3   Ireland has one of most advanced telecommunications networks in Europe.

4   Employment costs in Germany are among the most high in the world.

5   The scenery is more spectacular that I expected.

6   Dublin is among the cosmopolitanest cities in Europe.

7   There are good reasons for relocating, but there are even more better reasons for relocating to Ireland.

8   Employment costs are less high as in other European countries.

9   Come to Ireland. You'll settle in even more quick as you thought.

10 Ireland is not the same that it was thirty years ago. It's the bigger surprise in Europe.

Complete the text with the following adjectives.

wide	easy	major	available
immediate	impressive	numerous	fast-growing

This office site, which is shared with an (1) _____ selection of companies and organisations, is prominently located in a (2) _____ corporate business area. There is (3) _____ access to public transport with (4) _____ bus routes servicing the area. Two underground stations are also within walking distance. In the (5) _____ area there is a (6) _____ range of bars and restaurants and most (7) _____ High Street shops. Staff facilities in the area are therefore excellent. These premises will be (8) _____ from early July.

Read through the tapescript. Find phrases which are useful in giving directions.

You work at the avenue Voltaire site. A client is visiting you next week for the first time and needs directions. Write an e-mail giving directions from the metro station to the office.

Complete the conversation. Write in the missing questions.

● Hello, David? It's Simon Fletcher again.

▼ Hello, Simon. So what did you think of the property?

● Very impressive. There are just a few details I'd like to check first.

▼ OK. What do you want to know?

● (1) _____

▼ Well, it should be free on 1 August.

● Good. (2) _____

▼ Only the fifth and the sixth floors are free.

● OK. (3) _____

▼ Yes. There's a large underground car park for the building. And the public transport facilities are excellent. There are three underground stations nearby.

● (4) _____

▼ They're all only about 10 minutes' walk away.

● Right. (5) _____

▼ No problem. I'll get something off to you today.

5 Read through the unit. Find words connected with *facilities* and *amenities*.

air-conditioning   passenger lifts

(facilities and amenities)

6 Complete the sentences with the following words.

renovation	square metres	premises	tenant
appointment	property	location	

1 The last _____ left the place in a terrible condition.

2 Viewing is by _____ only through the official agents.

3 There's still a little _____ work to be done on the outside of the building.

4 The office is in an excellent central _____ .

5 Where are your new _____ ?

6 Each of the offices measures approximately 40 _____ .

7 This _____ should be available soon.

Participles

7 **Form adjectives from the following verbs. Then complete each sentence with a suitable adjective.**

shock	confuse	excite
disappoint	interest	fascinate

1 I'm very _____ about the new offices. They look fantastic.

2 The terms of the lease are very _____ . Can you explain them to me?

3 We're very _____ in the office site we saw.

4 We're very _____ that the building won't be free till June. You said it'd be free in March.

5 We were _____ when he told us the rent. I couldn't believe it would be so high.

6 It's a _____ old building with lots of character.

Listening Test Part One

Questions 1 - 12

- You will hear three telephone conversations.
- Write **one or two** words or a number in the numbered space on the forms below.
- You will hear each conversation twice.

Conversation One
(Questions 1 - 4)

- Look at the form below.
- You will hear a man giving information about a training course.

Telephone message

For: David   **Taken by:** Joanna   **Date:** 1.8.99   **Time:** 5pm

Peter Carver rang about the **(1)** ....*training course*.... you're interested in. It's called

(2) ....*managing people*.... and the next one is on **(3)** ....*13 August*....

If you're interested, call Virginia Little on 01723 **(4)** ....*01723 88 7752*.... (4)

Conversation Two
(Questions 5 - 8)

- Look at the form below.
- You will hear a man booking a taxi.

Longside Taxis   Booking form

Date: 13.5.99

Booking taken by: Julia   **Customer name:** Wentworth Engineering

Pick-up time: **(5)** ....*4.30*....

Passenger name: Susan **(6)** ....*BRIGHTON ROUGHTON*....

Destination: **(7)** ....*Airport gatwick*.... (3)

Pick-up from: Wentworth Engineering (passenger at the **(8)** ....*Reception*....)

Conversation Three
(Questions 9 - 12)

- Look at the form below.
- You will hear a man giving information about a talk.

Ridgeway Park
Management Institute

OUTSIDE SPEAKER BOOKING SHEET

NAME OF SPEAKER: Dr Alan Barker

ORGANISATION: Institute of European Management Consultants

TITLE OF TALK: (9) ....measuring.....performance.....1

DATE/TIME: 19th March 1999, 9.30 am
②

VENUE: (10) .....conference.....room...., Ridgeway Park Management Institute   2

EQUIPMENT: Whiteboard, VCR, (11) ....CD player casset player

FEE: (12) ....£ 2 50

Listening Test Part Two

Questions 13 - 22

Section One
(Questions 13 - 17)

- You will hear five people talking about different items of office equipment.
- For each piece, decide which item **A - H** the speaker is talking about.
- Write **one** letter **A - H** next to the number of the piece.
- Do not use any letter more than once.
- You will hear the five pieces twice.

A	answering machine
B	cassette player
C	fax machine
D	overhead projector
E	paper shredder
F	photocopier
G	printer
H	video player

13 B ✓

14 ~~E~~ F

15 A ✓   ②

16 ~~A~~ E

17 C ✓

Section Two
(Questions 18 - 22)

- You will hear another five short pieces.
- For each piece, decide what the speaker is trying to do.
- Write one letter **A - H** next to the number of the piece.
- Do not use any letter more than once.
- You will hear the five pieces twice.

18 *B....* N

19 *G...* ✓   ③

20 *F....* ✓

21 *Ø.E*

22 *C...* ✓

A	place an order
B	make a complaint
C	change an appointment
D	give a warning
E	explain a delay
F	thank someone
G	make an announcement
H	reject an offer

Listening Test Part Three

Questions 23 - 30

- You will hear a report about Vie Vitale, a manufacturer of health and beauty products.
- For each question **23 - 30**, choose one letter (**A**, **B**, or **C**) for the correct answer.
- You will hear the report twice.

23 How many jobs are likely to be lost at Vie Vitale?

   A 200
   B 300
   C 500

24 Jobs cuts are not expected in

   A manufacturing.
   B distribution.
   C product development.

25 Vie Vitale is in a difficult situation because

   A their ideas are no longer unique.
   B the market sector is no longer fashionable.
   C competitors now have cheaper products.

26 La Face announced it is going to

   A develop its own retail outlets.
   B concentrate on mail order sales.
   C sell through department stores.

27 As a result of restructuring, Vie Vitale's share price is now

   A lower than at the start of the year.

   B the same as the start of the year.

   C higher than at the start of the year.

28 How does Vie Vitale intend to win back its market leadership?

   A By bringing out new products.

   B By changing its basic approach.

   C By modernising its image.

29 What is Vie Vitale's strategy concerning its shops?

   A It is reducing the number of its shops.

   B It is buying back more of its outlets.

   C It is creating more franchises.

30 Vie Vitale owns all of its shops in

   A France.

   B Germany.

   C the UK.

Reading Test Part Five

Section A

- Read the extract from a book review.
- In most lines **1 - 5** there is **one extra word** which does not fit in. One or two lines, however, are correct.
- If a line is correct, write **CORRECT**.
- If there is an extra word in the line, write the **extra word in CAPITAL LETTERS**.

Example

0   `C` `O` `R` `R` `E` `C` `T` `☐` `☐`

00 `O` `F` `☐` `☐` `☐` `☐` `☐` `☐` `☐`

0   This book, the latest addition to the 60-minute self-learning series, is filled

00 with assessments as well as case studies from both of the employees' and

1   managers' viewpoints. It begins by defining the term coaching, and explains

2   that it is a process used up by managers to prepare employees for the

3   realities of the workplace and to help with the employees handle

4   problems related to work performance. The framework for a personal

5   action plan is very helpful and as is the final assessment

    task. Overall, this is an excellent introduction to a highly important subject.

The Reading Test

Overview

The Reading Test has five parts testing various reading skills. Part Four specifically tests a candidate's knowledge of vocabulary.

Part	Input	Task
1	Four 60 word texts	Matching sentences with texts
2	500-600 word text	Sentence level gap-filling
3	400-500 word text	Matching headings with paragraphs Completing sentence stems
4	250 word text	Single word multiple-choice gap-filling
5a	80-100 word text	Identifying extra words
5b	80-100 word text	Correcting mistakes

Length: The Reading Test is part of the Reading and Writing paper, which lasts 90 minutes. You should allow 50-60 minutes for the Reading Test.

How to succeed

Here are some important tips for doing the Reading Test.

- Read all instructions **carefully.**
- Read through the whole text once before looking at the questions.
- Underline the answers in the text - it will make checking quicker.
- The questions are generally in the same order as the answers. If you are confident that an answer is right, continue from that point in the text, not from the beginning.
- Leave difficult questions and return to them later if you have time.
- Only write **one** answer for each question.
- **Never** leave a question unanswered. If you run out of time or have no idea, guess.
- Leave enough time for the Writing Test. It represents 25% of the final mark.
- Use any time you have left to check your answers.

The reading tasks

❶ Part One tests the ability to read for both gist and specific information. Look at the text and the three sentences below. Which sentence matches the text best? Underline the parts of the text which help you to identify the correct option.

> We are looking for an experienced International Business Development Manager to represent a leading London-based package holiday company. Duties will include dealing with partners throughout Europe. Applicants will be fluent in two European languages, possess good word-processing skills and be familiar with databases. Competitive basic salary, health insurance and company car.

1   The job requires a working knowledge of computer software.
2   The company is specifically looking for European applicants.
3   The advertisement emphasises the amount of travelling required.

❷ Part Two tests the ability to ensure that the overall meaning of a text is clear and that the parts of the text are logically linked. Look at the extract and the three sentences below. Which sentence fills the gap best? Why do the other sentences not fit?

> Normally, you would expect price to be the only important issue when selling a company. If the owner of a business decides to sell, it is usually in order to get as much cash from the sale as possible. But it is not always the case. **(1)** ..... . However much might be offered, the owners could refuse to sell, especially if the new owner would then use the company to take market share from the former parent company.

A   With sales of family firms, the family often feels it does not want to be exploited.
B   If an organisation is selling a subsidiary, for example, it is unlikely to sell to a competitor.
C   To get around this, the value of the company can be set by an independent auditor.

❸ Part Three is in two sections. Section A tests the ability to read for gist. Look at the paragraph and the three titles below. Which title matches the paragraph best? Underline any words in the paragraph which might encourage you to select an incorrect option.

> The company's decline began four years ago. It was generally assumed that the video rental business was dying because of the availability of video on demand supplied by satellite and cable television companies. But in reality it was poor store management not technology that was at the heart of customer dissatisfaction and the company's poor performance. It was this that resulted in customers renting fewer videos, a declining membership and the company announcing in 1999 that profits had fallen by over 20 per cent, despite the fact that the market was still actually growing.

A   Misunderstanding the market
B   Identifying the problem
C   Meeting customer needs

4 Section B of Part Three tests the ability to read for specific information. Read the text again and look at the sentence stem. Which option completes the sentence best?

1 The company was losing business due to ...
  A new technology such as video on demand.
  B a decline in the video rental market.
  C the way its shops were run.

5 Part Four tests vocabulary. Candidates have to choose the correct word from a set of four options to fill each gap in a text. Look at the extract below and the options. Which is the best option to fill each gap? In what contexts are the other options possible?

> The most common complaints about meetings are that there are no clear objectives, they do not stick to the **(1)** ..... , they go on too long and are often **(2)** ..... at short notice after all the preparation work has already been done.

1 A itinerary   B agenda   C plan   D timetable
2 A cancelled   B stopped   C delayed   D prevented

6 Part Five is in two sections. Section A tests the ability to proof-read a short text in which several lines include an extra word. However, some lines are correct. Look at the following text and underline the extra words in the numbered lines. Why are they incorrect?

> 1 First, let me apologise you for the late delivery of your order and the
> 2 problems you experienced trying to get in contact with us. This was due
> 3 to the installation of our new telephone system, which it meant our
>   phones were out of operation on several occasions last week.

Exam tip:
Concentrate on small grammatical words such as articles, pronouns and prepositions.

7 Section B of Part Five tests a candidate's knowledge of grammar and vocabulary. In this section there is an incorrect word in every numbered line. Correct the mistakes in the text below.

> 1 UniChip, the Japan computer manufacturer, has announced that it is to
> 2 build a new £200m production facility at Scotland. The factory will create
> 3 300 jobs in the Glasgow area and near double output. Building will start
>   next month and be completed early next year.

The Listening Test

Overview

The Listening Test has three parts.

Part	Input	Task
I	3 short telephone conversations	Gap-filling (words and numbers)
2	2 sets of 5 short monologues	Matching monologues with topics/places etc. Matching monologues with functions
3	A longer conversation or monologue (3-4 minutes)	Multiple-choice comprehension questions

Length: A total of 12 minutes of listening material played twice, plus 10 minutes at the end to transfer answers to the Answer Sheet.

Before listening

1 It is important that you use your time well **before** you listen. Here are some tips.

- Read the instructions **very carefully** before you listen.
- Check the type of answer you need to give. Is it words or numbers?
- Check the number of words you should write for each answer.
- You will always be given time to read through the questions before you listen. Use this time well. Try to predict words you might hear and what the answers might be.

2 Work in pairs. Look at the form below from Part One of a Listening Test. Predict words that might fill the gaps and complete the form.

- Look at the note below.
- You will hear someone making a call about a form that has not been filled in correctly.

MESSAGE

To: Jane Mahoney
Date: 10 March

Paul Charles from the **(1)** .... Department called. He's returning your **(2)** .... from your trip to Brazil. He said it needs **(3)** .... from the Department Head. When you've got it, could you return the completed form **(4)** ....?

While listening

❶ Always listen carefully to the whole recording. Don't choose your answer too quickly! The recording often deliberately contains words from the incorrect options.

Look at the tapescript below. Which of the managers A-C is speaking? Why might some candidates choose a wrong option in this case?

A Sales Manager	B Production Manager	C Transport Manager

> Well, sales have been exceptionally good for the last few months, so everyone's been very busy. I don't know how they've done it, but somehow Production's managed to keep up with all these extra orders. But it's not so easy for us. Our fleet is already operating at the limit. I simply don't have enough lorries to get everything out of the warehouse quickly enough.

After listening

❶ Always check your answers very carefully. Look at the question papers below. Find the candidate's mistakes.

PART ONE
- You will hear three telephone conversations.
- Write **one or two words or a number** in the numbered spaces on each form.
- You will hear each conversation twice.

Conversation One
(Questions 1-4)

Mr   **(1)** ....

Called at: **(2)** *3.00 in the afternoon*

PART TWO
- You will hear five people talking about their jobs.
- For each piece decide who is speaking **A-H**.
- Write **one** letter **A-H** next to the number of the piece.
- Do not use any letter more than once.
- You will hear the five pieces twice.

13 *B/C*

14 *B*

A	Sales Manager
B	Production Manager
C	Transport Manager

PART THREE
- Listen to a radio report about a merger.
- For each question **23-30**, mark the correct letter **A, B or C**.
- You will hear the conversation twice.

23 The two companies merged because they
   Ⓐ were too small to be individually competitive.
   B their product ranges matched each other.
   Ⓒ thought it would significantly reduce their costs.

The Speaking Test

Overview

The Speaking Test takes place with two, or possibly three, candidates and two examiners. The first examiner speaks to the candidates. The second examiner listens and assesses the candidates' English.

Part	Format	Input	Task
I	Examiner talks to each candidate individually	Examiner asks questions	Speaking about yourself Responding to questions Giving longer responses
2a	Candidate talks to candidate	Written prompt	Exchanging information
2b	Candidate talks to candidate	Written prompt	Discussing a topic

Length: A total of 12 minutes. Part 1 lasts 3-4 minutes and Part 2 lasts 7-8 minutes. Interviews with three candidates will be slightly longer.

How to succeed

The Speaking Test assesses candidates' performance in a number of areas. Here are some important tips for each area.

Interactive communication
- Listen carefully to all instructions.
- Ask the examiner to repeat any instructions you are not sure about.
- Give full appropriate answers, not just one or two words.
- Keep to and complete the task. Do not talk about other things.
- Good communication means working with and helping the other candidate. Remember, you are not in competition with the other candidate.

Linking of ideas
Take a moment to organise your ideas before you speak. You can link your ideas in several ways, such as:
- sequence (e.g. *first of all, then, after that*)
- importance (e.g. *I think the most important thing is ...*)
- contrast (e.g. *but, although*).

Grammar and vocabulary
- You will be marked on both accuracy and range. It is therefore important to show variety in your language. However, do not be over-ambitious!

Pronunciation
- Speak clearly and at a natural speed.

Personal information

1 After introducing him/herself, the examiner will check that the information on each candidate's entry form is correct. He/she will then ask candidates a few general questions about themselves. Write three questions for each of the topics below.

your job/studies	places to live
free time	transport

Now work in pairs. Ask and answer questions about the topics.

Listening **2** Listen to Sagrario and Max doing Part One of a Speaking Test. Read the exam tips again and listen to the test. What do they do wrong?

Candidate 1   Candidate 2

Examiner 1

Examiner 2

Interview One, Part One

Sagrario _____

Max _____

3 Now listen to the same candidates doing Part One of the test again. How is their performance better?

Interview Two, Part One

Sagrario _____

Max _____

Information exchange

1 Part Two A tests candidates' ability to exchange information with each other. Look at the information which the examiner gives Sagrario and Max, which you can find on pages 149 and 150. What questions should Sagrario and Max ask?

2 Look at the following tips.

- Check that the other candidate is ready to start.
- Be polite, friendly and helpful to the other candidate.
- Ask the other candidate to repeat anything that is not clear.
- Thank the other candidate when the task is complete.

What phrases would it be useful to add to the questions in the information exchange?

Listening ❸ Listen to Sagrario and Max doing Part Two A of the Speaking Test. What do they do wrong?

te 1 ◄───► Candidate 2

Examiner 1

r 2

Interview One, Part Two A

Sagrario _____

Max _____

❹ Now listen to the same candidates doing Part Two A again. In what way is their performance better?

Interview Two, Part Two A

Sagrario _____

Max _____

Speaking ❺ Now practise Part Two A of the Speaking Test. Student A: Look at the information on page 148. Student B: Look at the information on page 151.

Discussion

Speaking ❶ In Part Two B of the Speaking Test the candidates are given a topic to discuss for about three minutes. This tests candidates' ability to exchange opinions and interact with each other. What phrases could you use to do the following?

- give your opinion
- encourage the other candidate to speak
- ask the other candidate to clarify his/her ideas
- disagree politely with the other candidate

Listening ❷ Now listen to two versions of Sagrario and Max discussing the topic on pages 149 and 150. How do they interact with each other? What is the difference between the two versions?

Speaking ❸ Work in pairs. Look at the information at the bottom of pages 148 and 151. Discuss the topic with your partner. In the exam you will have thirty seconds to think about what you want to say before you begin.

The Writing Test

Overview

The Writing Test has two questions.

Part	Input	Task
1	Instructions	Writing a short memo or note (30-40 words)
2	Letter, memo or note	Writing a letter or short report (100-120 words)

Length: The Writing Test is part of the Reading and Writing Paper, which lasts 90 minutes. You should allow at least 30 minutes for the Writing Test.

How to succeed

The Writing Test assesses candidates' performance in a number of areas: task completion, organisation of ideas, appropriateness, range of vocabulary and accuracy of grammar and spelling.

Task
- Successful task completion means fulfilling all parts of the task appropriately. Even a grammatically perfect answer may still get a low mark if it does not include all the necessary information.
- Keep to the word limit. If you are below it, you have probably not fully completed the task. If you are above it, you have probably included unnecessary information.

Language
- Task completion is so important that you can get high marks even with minor language mistakes.
- Show a range of vocabulary, where possible. Try not to repeat words.
- You can organise your ideas in several ways, such as:
    - addition (e.g. *also, as well, furthermore*)
    - contrast (e.g. *but, although, however*)
    - sequence (e.g. *first of all, then, after that*).
- Use headings, paragraphs and bullet points to improve clarity in memos and reports.
- Use language which is appropriate to the type of writing. Short forms, e.g. *I'm*, are acceptable in notes and some memos but not in formal letters or reports.
- Check your writing **carefully** when you have finished.

Memos and notes

1 Work in pairs. Look at the Part One task and the three sample answers below. What mistakes have the candidates made? Put the samples in order from best to worst.

Question 46

• You are the manager of a small export company. Pedro Fernández, an important client, is visiting your company for three days from 22 October.

• Write a note of **30 - 40 words** to your secretary:

  * asking her to book a hotel room
  * saying where the hotel should be
  * giving her the dates.

• Write on your Answer Sheet.

Candidate A

> Dear Ms Jones
>   I am writing to inform you of the visit of Mr Pedro Fernández. Would you please be so kindly as to reserve a suitable hotel room for him.
>
>   Yours sincerelly

Candidate B

> Hi Mary
> Look, I'm really sorry to troubel you, but Mr Fernández - a really important client - will visit the company for three days from 22 October to discuss a contract with us. Please will you book for Mr Fernández a really nice hotel room as soon as possible. Thanks very much.
>
>   Cheers !

Candidate C

> Mary
> Could you please hire a hotel room for three nights for Mr Pedro Fernández, who is visiting us on 22 October. The hotel should be somewhere in the centre of town.
>   Thank you.

2 Read the tips below. Then do the writing task on the Activity sheet on page 147.

• Read all instructions **carefully**. Do you need to write a memo or a note? This will have an effect on the formality of your language.
• Check you have completed all three parts of the task. Use the instructions as a checklist.
• Check the length of your first draft and edit if necessary.
• Proof-read your answer carefully to check grammar, vocabulary and style.

Formal letters

1 In Part Two of the Writing Test candidates may be asked to write a formal letter. Read the task and look at the suggested procedure below.

Question 47

- You are the owner of a clothing factory. A customer has sent you a letter summarising a recent negotiation. You have written some notes on the letter.
- Write a **100 - 120 word** reply to the buyer using the letter and your notes.
- Do not include addresses.

Mrs P Mirza
Lahore Textiles
6 Ocean Road
Lahore

Dear Parveen

So are we!

It was good to see you again last week and we are delighted that your silk blouses will be included in our winter catalogue.

As promised, listed below are the points agreed at the meeting. *Which colours?*

1 The contract is for the Sheba range of silk blouses in three colours.

2 You will grant us exclusive import rights for the blouses in the UK.

3 The quantity will be 5,000 pieces, with a further option of 3,000. *We agreed 4,0*

4 The price per piece will be $5.65 for the first 5,000. You will confirm the price for the optional 3,000 pieces. *$5.25 for the optional pieces*

5 Payment will be by letter of credit.

6 The initial order will be ready ex factory by 1 August 1999.

Not possible - 15th at the earliest

I trust you will find this in order. I look forward to your written confirmation in due course.

Best regards

Stephanie Powell
Chief Purchaser

---

1 Plan your answer. How many paragraphs will there be? What is the purpose of each one?
2 Think of key phrases and vocabulary to include in the paragraphs.
3 Check that your plan covers all five points. Then write your answer.
4 Check your answer.
   - *Does it fully complete the task?*
   - *Is the information clearly organised?*
   - *Are the grammar, vocabulary and style correct?*
5 Make any necessary changes. Make sure you keep within 100-120 words.

2 Look at the model answer below. The five points in task are highlighted in blue.

Begin your letter with an appropriate salutation.

Do not use short forms in a formal business letter.

...ide your letter ...arly into paragraphs. ...h one should ...oduce a new idea.

...se numbers and ...llet points to make ...e layout clear.

...se linking words to ...nnect ideas.

...ake sure you finish ...th an appropriate ...osing sentence.

Dear Stephanie

Thank you for your letter of 12.1.99. We are delighted that the Sheba range will be in your catalogue.

There are, however, some small points which need clarifying.

- The Sheba range comes in six colours. Please look at the samples and confirm which three colours you would like.

- You referred to the further option of 3,000 pieces. I thought we had agreed on 4,000. Please confirm the correct figure.

- I can confirm the optional pieces will cost $5.25 each.

Unfortunately, due to a full order book, we are unable to deliver by 1.8.99. The earliest date would be 15.8.99. I hope this will be acceptable.

I look forward to hearing from you soon.

Regards

Use an appropriate closure which matches the salutation.

3 Here are some useful phrases for formal business letters.

Referring to previous contact

Thank you for	your letter of/dated ...
With reference to	
Further to	
In reply to	

Stating the reason for writing

I am writing	to enquire about ...
	to confirm that ...
	to apologise for/about ...
	in reply to your ...
	with reference to ...

Ending a letter

If you have any further questions, please contact me on ...

I look forward to hearing from you	soon.
	in due course.
	in the near future.

Letters of enquiry

I am writing to enquire about ...
I am interested in your ...
I would be very grateful if you could send me ...
I would like further information about ...

Letters of apology

I am writing to apologise for/about ...
This was due to ...
Unfortunately, we have been unable to ...
I am sorry for any inconvenience this has caused.
I can assure you that we will ...

Letters of complaint

I am writing to complain about ...
I am not satisfied with ...
I must therefore insist that ...

Reports

❶ In Part Two of the Writing Test candidates may be asked to write a short report. Read the task and look at the suggested procedure below.

Question 47
- You work for a company that sells electrical goods. You have recently visited a potential supplier in Slovakia. Look at the memo and your handwritten notes.
- Write a **100 - 120 word** report recommending whether your company should deal with the supplier or not.

To: Alan
From: Georgina
Date: 16 February 2000
Re: Your visit to Ludova Technologies Slovensko

Alan

Here's the information about Ludova Technologies. It isn't much, I'm afraid, but it's all we have.

The company is 15 years old and employs about 20 people. It's located in the south west of Slovakia, on the Austrian border. They make electrical goods such as pocket radios, but we're not really sure what else.

Can you find out the following and write a report recommending what we should do?

(Don't forget to make a final recommendation)

The factory
- What are the production facilities like? — (Old equipment, but modernisation planned)
- What is the production capacity? — (Quite low due to old machines)

Products
- What is the product range like? — (Wide range, good quality)

Production times
- How quickly can they deliver? — (Long delivery times - explain why)

Your flight and hotel are booked and Mr Pavol Kukura will meet you at the airport on Friday. Good luck!

1   Plan your report. How many sections will there be? Give each section a heading.
2   Think of phrases and vocabulary to include in each section.
3   Check that your plan covers all five points. Then write your report.
4   Check your answer.
- *Does it fully complete the task?*
- *Is the information clearly organised?*
- *Are the grammar, vocabulary and style appropriate?*
5   Make any necessary changes. Make sure you keep within 100-120 words.

2 Look at the model answer below. The five points in the task are highlighted in blue.

he report needs to
e clearly divided
to sections. Each
ection requires a
uitable heading.

Always give the
report an overall title.

Use abbreviations for
names to reduce the
number of words.

Report on suitability of Ludova Technologies Slovensko (LTS)

Introduction

Where possible, use
andard phrases.

This report aims to assess whether the Slovakian company Ludova Technologies would be a suitable supplier of electrical goods.

Findings

A recent visit to the company showed that its facilities are quite old, resulting in a limited production capacity. Despite this, LTS produces an extensive range of high-quality products including radios, cassette recorders and CD players.

se linking words to
onnect ideas.

However, out-of-date machinery means delivery times of up to three months. This may change when the planned modernisation takes place.

Conclusion

se formal language
nd no short forms.

LTS would not be suitable for large orders that require quick delivery.

Recommendations

It is recommended that we remain in contact with LTS and reconsider a supply contract once the factory modernisation is completed.

Keep introductions, conclusions
and recommendations to just
one sentence.

3 Here are some useful phrases for report writing.

Introduction
The aim/purpose of this report is to ...
This report aims to
This report sets out to ...

Findings
It was found that ...
... clearly show(s) that ...

Conclusion(s)
It was concluded/decided/agreed/felt that ...
No conclusions were reached regarding the ...
In conclusion/On balance, ...

Recommendation(s)
We would recommend that ...
It is recommended/proposed/suggested that ...

Adding ideas
Furthermore/Moreover/In addition, ...

Contrasting ideas
However, ...
Although ...
Despite/In spite of ...
... while/whereas ...

Making comparisons
Both/Neither ...
Like/Unlike ...

Linking cause and effect
because of/as a result of/due to/owing to ...
This means ...
... leads to/results in ...

Reporting results

Measuring performance

Speaking ❶ What information is used to measure the performance of a company? Where can you find this information?

Listening ❷ Listen to a television report about Budgens, a supermarket chain. Which of the following are mentioned? Did they rise or fall?

profit	turnover	share price	sales volume	dividend

❸ Listen again and answer the questions below.

1 What is Budgens' current strategy? Give examples.
2 How successful is TeleShop Services?
3 Why did Budgens' share price rise so quickly?
4 What helped the share price at the start of this year?

4 Listen again to the second half of the report and complete the graph below.

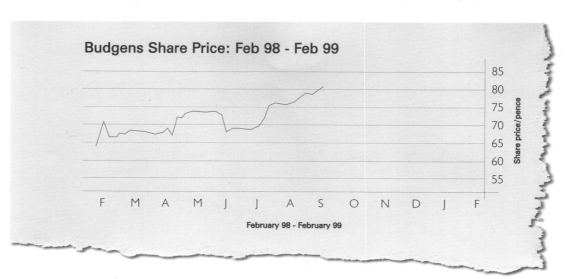

Budgens Share Price: Feb 98 - Feb 99

F M A M J J A S O N D J F

February 98 - February 99

Share price / pence: 85 80 75 70 65 60 55

Vocabulary **5** Look at the tapescript. Find verbs to describe the pictures below. Then write the noun form for each verb.

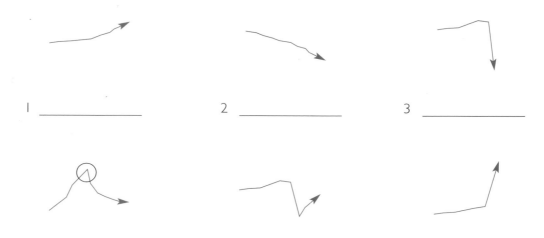

1 _____

2 _____

3 _____

4 _____

5 _____

6 _____

Speaking **6** Work in pairs. Student A: Look at the Activity sheet on page 146. Student B: Look at the Activity sheet on page 153.

Annual reports

Reading ❶ Look at the following extracts from the Chairman's Statement in four annual reports. Which extract does each sentence below refer to?

'88 '89 '90 '91 '92 '93 '94 '95 '96 '97

A   Strike action and unfavourable exchange rates led to losses that were almost balanced by gains from our ongoing resource efficiency programme, which delivered an impressive £100m of cost performance improvements. Another source of revenue was the recent disposal of Dennox, our wholly-owned subsidiary.

B   The company made steady progress, with profits before tax and exceptional items increasing to £596m. Careful cash management continues to be a major feature of the company's strong performance. Despite pressures from increased investment activity, the balance sheet shows net cash at £3.2bn after expenditure of £346m.

C   Trading volume increased by 4.5%, which was well up on recent years, and turnover rose by 3%. Operating margins also increased, as a result of the restructuring programme that was completed at the end of last year. Although successful, the programme meant a reduction in net cash to £472m.

D   Our major achievement last year was the £4.8bn acquisition of a speciality chemicals business. This investment, along with the planned sale of assets, will help streamline the company's range of businesses. Trading profit fell by 7% due to disappointments in non-core activities, confirming the logic of the actions we are taking.

1 The company enjoyed a substantial increase in its sales.
2 The company offset some of its poor trading results by selling assets.
3 The Chairman explains why substantial investment was necessary.
4 The Chairman refers to the success of previous organisational changes.
5 The company's cost-cutting measures are proving very successful.
6 The Chairman refers to the company's success in controlling new spending.
7 The company is currently implementing a major transformation programme.

Speaking ❷ Which company has the best results? Which has the worst?

Vocabulary ❸ Read the extracts again. Underline words and phrases which link cause and effect. Think of other words and phrases you could use in their place.

Speaking **4** Work in pairs. Your company has a large cash surplus and wants to invest in shares. Look at the information about Ramsden Breweries plc and Bute Chemicals plc. Which company would you invest in?

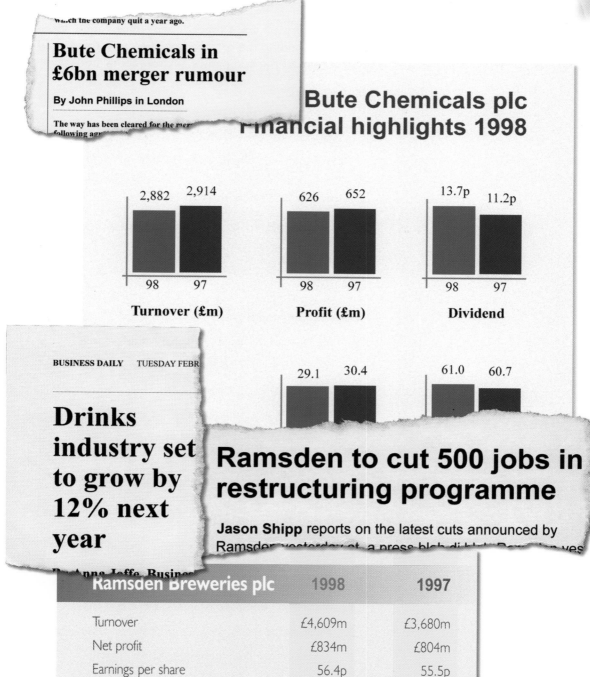

w...ch the company quit a year ago.

Bute Chemicals in £6bn merger rumour

By John Phillips in London

The way has been cleared for the mer
following agr

Bute Chemicals plc
Financial highlights 1998

| 2,882 | 2,914 | | 626 | 652 | | 13.7p | 11.2p |

| 98 | 97 | | 98 | 97 | | 98 | 97 |

Turnover (£m)   **Profit (£m)**   **Dividend**

BUSINESS DAILY   TUESDAY FEBR

Drinks industry set to grow by 12% next year

By Anne Jaffa Busine

| 29.1 | 30.4 | | 61.0 | 60.7 |

Ramsden to cut 500 jobs in restructuring programme

Jason Shipp reports on the latest cuts announced by
Ramsden

Ramsden Breweries plc	1998	1997
Turnover	£4,609m	£3,680m
Net profit	£834m	£804m
Earnings per share	56.4p	55.5p
Dividend per share	30p	29p

Writing **5** Write a 100-120 word report comparing the two companies and recommending the most suitable for investment. Before you write, think carefully about the following.

- How many parts will the report have?
- What heading will each part have?
- What information will each part contain?

Environmental report

Assessing environmental impact

Speaking ❶ Work in pairs. Find out the following information about your partner's company. Add up the total score. Then turn to page 147 for an assessment of the company's environmental impact.

Western College of Higher Education

Environmental Questionnaire

As part of our research into environmental practices in local offices, we kindly ask employers to complete this questionnaire, which will be collected on ___Tuesday___ .

Please tick (✓) the boxes if the following statements are true of general office practice at your company.

Waste management

☐	We have formal waste management guidelines.	+3
☐	We separate all waste for collection and recycling.	+2
☐	We use recycled paper and envelopes.	+3
☐	We re-use paper in the office.	+1

Energy consumption

☐	We have a formal energy consumption policy.	+3
☐	We use energy-efficient computer hardware.	+2
☐	We use low-energy lighting.	+2
☐	The office uses no energy outside working hours.	+1

Transport

☐	We provide transport for our employees.	+3
☐	We subsidise employees' use of public transport.	+2
☐	We encourage the organisation of car sharing.	+1

Total

Thank you for your co-operation.

❷ Think of three things your company could do to reduce its impact on the environment.

Environmental performance

Listening ❶ Geoff Paddock, Senior Group Press Officer at ICI (Imperial Chemicals Industries), gives a presentation to potential investors on the company's environmental performance. Listen and choose one letter for the correct answer.

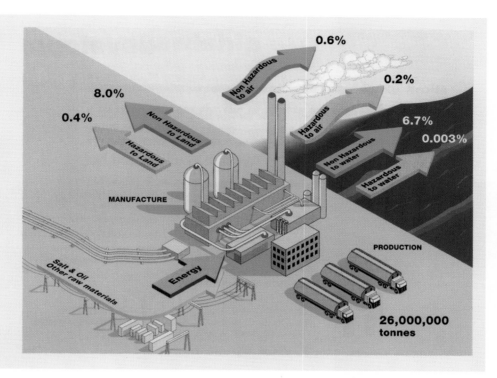

Wastes compared with output

Our hazardous waste constitutes only 0.55 per cent by volume of our output - everything we make and sell - which we estimate was ... million tonnes in 1995.

This diagram shows the routes of disposal of wastes expressed as a percentage of our total output.

1 ICI's environmental project was a response to
   A shareholder demands.
   B public pressure.
   C government legislation.

2 Between 1990 and 1995, ICI's environmental investment totalled about
   A £200 million.
   B £500 million.
   C £1 billion.

3 ICI concentrated expenditure on problems that
   A were the cheapest to solve.
   B could be fixed quickly.
   C would make the most difference.

4 By 2000 all ICI business will meet
   A internationally recognised environmental regulations.
   B local environmental regulations throughout the world.
   C the company's own environmental regulations.

5 By 2000 ICI will have reduced its energy consumption by
   A 10% per year.
   B 10% of the 1990 figure.
   C 10% of the 1995 figure.

6 ICI will halve its environmental impact by concentrating on the
   A most dangerous types of waste.
   B number of different types of waste.
   C more common types of waste.

7 The Product Stewardship Programmes will
   A inform the public about all product life cycles.
   B improve information about chemicals used by the company.
   C become a standard part of the company's annual report.

8 Geoff Paddock believes that complying with future environmental legislation will
   A become much more difficult for the company.
   B be easier if the company makes changes now.
   C help the company to influence government policy.

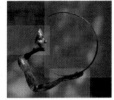

The Challenge 2000 symbol

Speaking **2** Summarise the four main points of the Challenge 2000 project. Which would make the most difference to the environment? Put them in order.

3 How can companies balance the interests of customers and shareholders with a commitment to the environment?

Vocabulary **4** Complete the information below with phrases from the tapescript.

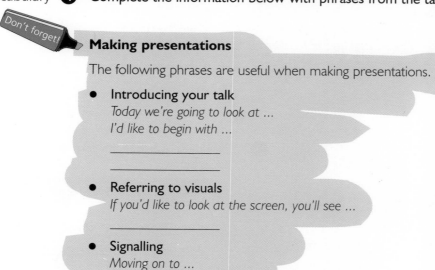

Don't forget!

Making presentations

The following phrases are useful when making presentations.

- **Introducing your talk**
  Today we're going to look at ...
  I'd like to begin with ...
  _____
  _____

- **Referring to visuals**
  If you'd like to look at the screen, you'll see ...
  _____

- **Signalling**
  Moving on to ...
  _____

Speaking **5** Work in groups. Look at the information below. Prepare a brief presentation on the company's environmental performance.

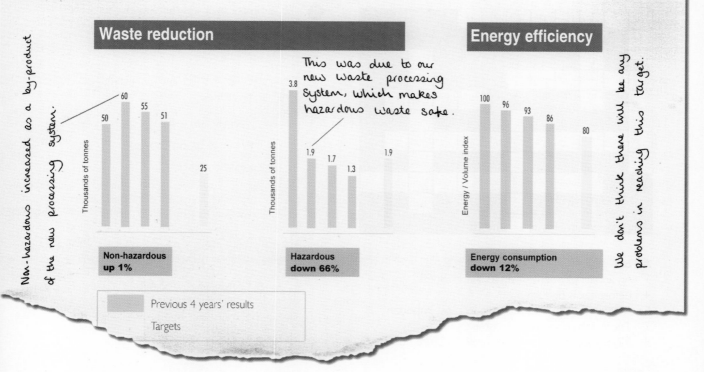

Here's the information you wanted about waste reduction and energy efficiency. The figures show the last four years and our planned targets for the end of next year. I'm afraid we don't have this year's figures yet. Good luck with the presentation!

All the best, Jo

Waste reduction

Non-hazardous increased as a by-product of the new processing system.

Thousands of tonnes

50 60 55 51 25

Non-hazardous up 1%

This was due to our new waste processing system, which makes hazardous waste safe.

3.8

Thousands of tonnes

1.9 1.7 1.3 1.9

Hazardous down 66%

Energy efficiency

Energy / Volume index

100 96 93 86 80

Energy consumption down 12%

We don't think there will be any problems in reaching this target.

Previous 4 years' results

Targets

Writing **6** Now write a short report on the company's performance. Write 100–120 words.

❶ Complete the description of the graph with the correct form of the following verbs.

recover	peak	fall	shoot up	collapse	rise

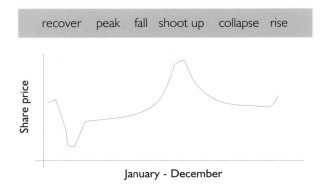

Share price

January - December

The share price (1) _____ slightly at the start of the year but (2) _____ in February. Shares then rose again and levelled off over the following quarter before (3) _____ in the summer. In August they finally (4) _____ and then started to (5) _____ steadily, dropping back to their spring level by the end of November. Rumours of good trading results led to a slight (6) _____ in the last few weeks, which returned shares to the same level as at the start of the year.

❷ Complete the crossword.

	¹d	i	v	i	d	e	n	d		

(crossword grid with numbered cells 1, 2, 3, 4, 5, 6, 7, 8)

Across
1 An annual payment made to shareholders
4 Before tax is deducted
5 A company's ..... activities are its most important
7 The purchase of another company
8 Money spent now in order to bring future benefit

Down
1 The sale of a subsidiary
2 ..... profit = profit after costs have been deducted
3 The sales of a company
6 The things a company owns which have value

❸ Complete each sentence with a suitable preposition.

1 The shares peaked _____ 260p in September.
2 Sales fell _____ £5.6m _____ £4.8m.
3 There was a decrease _____ net profit.
4 Sales rose _____ £2m. This was a rise _____ approximately 4%.

❹ Use these words in the correct form to connect the ideas below.

lead to	due to	mean	as a result of

1 sharp fall in profits ⇐ long strike
   There was a sharp fall in profits due to a long strike.

2 favourable exchange rate ⇒ increase in profits
   _____

3 sales fell ⇐ bad weather in the summer
   _____

4 strong competition ⇒ reduction in margins
   _____

5 share price collapse ⇐ bad publicity
   _____

Adjectives and adverbs

❺ Complete each sentence with the correct form of the word in capital letters.

1 SUDDEN
   The share price _____ collapsed in the summer.

2 SUBSTANTIAL
   The annual report showed _____ losses last year.

3 STEADY
   Growth is looking _____ at the moment.

4 HARD
   They have been working very _____ recently.

5 MARGINAL
   Sales are _____ up on this time last year.

6 DRAMATIC
   It all looks _____ different now.

S. S

How many words can you find in the unit and the tapescript which go after the word *environmental*?

environmental   _performance_

        _____

        _____

        _____

        _____

Now use the words to complete the sentences.

1 ICI's environmental _____ is called SHE Challenge 2000.

2 The government will probably introduce tougher environmental _____ .

3 The company is trying to reduce its environmental _____ by half.

4 ICI's environmental _____ were a response to public concern.

5 People today are far more aware of environmental _____ .

6 The company spends about £200m improving its environmental _____ .

Match the verbs with a similar meaning. Then think of a noun to follow each pair of verbs.

1	influence	realise
2	comply with	affect *government policy*
3	concentrate	deal with
4	assess	fulfil
5	address	focus
6	recognise	evaluate

Complete each sentence with the correct form of the word in capital letters.

1 CONSUME

We're reducing our energy _____ .

2 SUBSIDY

We are asking for _____ public transport.

3 OBLIGE

Everyone has an environmental section in their annual report now. It's almost _____ .

4 COMPLY

We're hoping to achieve 100% _____ with all major government regulations.

5 THREATEN

The law is a _____ to our business.

6 HAZARD

We are reducing the _____ by-products arising from our production processes.

7 SPEND

We've substantially increased our _____ on waste reduction.

Determiners

4 Choose the correct word to fill each gap.

> To: All Heads of Department
> Re: Waste Management
>
> It has come to the board's notice that the company wastes far too (1) ..... paper in its offices and that not (2) ..... is being done to address (3) ..... situation. Therefore, the company has recently drawn up a formal waste management policy for (4) ..... offices in the group. In the future, (5) ..... Head of Department will be asked to write a brief waste management report (6) ..... month. The report will include (7) ..... detailed information about the previous month's progress and proposed targets for (8) ..... following month. The report will also give (9) ..... information about current practices for the collection and separation of waste. (10) ..... expenditure that arises from (11) ..... reports will be charged to each department's Health & Safety budget. We would like to thank you for your co-operation in (12) ..... matter.

	A		B		C
1	many		much		plenty
2	all		any		enough
3	that		this		these
4	all		each		any
5	a		each		all
6	any		all		every
7	much		enough		both
8	this		that		the
9	some		much		several
10	An		Any		This
11	these		those		them
12	that		this		any

Reading Test Part Four

- Read the advertisement below about a mobile phone company.
- Choose the correct word **A**, **B**, **C** or **D** to fill each gap.
- For each gap **1 - 15**, mark **one** letter **A**, **B**, **C** or **D**.

XCelfon - The future of global communications

XCelfon is fully committed to the research, development and manufacture of state-of-the-art equipment for global telecommunications. **(0)** A.. in over 50 international markets, the company now exports 87 per cent of its production. Our large full graphic displays **(1)** A... the use of various alphabets, including Chinese, and have won awards **(2)** B/A the world.

This success is a result of our extensive marketing strategy, which **(3)** D.. us in touch with the constantly changing **(4)** C.. of our customers. XCelfon designs its phones with its customers in **(5)** A.. . Our mobile phones are extremely user-friendly, have a long battery **(6)** D... and excellent voice quality. Produced to the highest quality **(7)** A... , each phone is thoroughly tested before being **(8)** A.. .

XCelfon has grown rapidly due to its **(9)** A.. to quality. Our investment record speaks for itself. Ten per cent of net sales are **(10)** C... in research and development, ensuring that the company **(11)** A... its position as market leader in mobile phone technology.

XCelfon products are the perfect **(12)** A.. of superb design and technological know-how. Each of our technical **(13)** C... helps make our products easier to use. One such unique **(14)** B. is the customiser menu, which allows users to **(15)** B.. only the most frequently needed functions in their own user menu.

Example

0   (A) Active   B   Fit   C   Physical   D   Energetic

A   B   C   D

	A		B		C		D	
1	A	make	B	allow	C	prepare	D	mean
2	A	throughout	(B)	over	C	about	D	within
3	A	holds	B	remains	C	stays	(D)	keeps
4	A	claims	(B)	calls	C	demands	D	enquiries
5	A	mind	B	thought	C	vision	(D)	sight
6	A	duration	B	course	C	time	D	life
7	A	standards	B	grades	(C)	marks	D	results
8	A	transferred	B	conveyed	(C)	given	D	dispatched
9	(A)	awareness	B	attention	C	consideration	D	intention
10	A	spent	B	paid	(C)	re-invested	D	supplied
11	(A)	maintains	B	provides	C	continues	D	supports
12	A	connection	B	unity	C	join	D	combination
13	A	introductions	B	modernisations	(C)	innovations	D	differences
14	A	character	B	feature	C	property	D	factor
15	A	prefer	B	select	C	limit	D	reduce

Reading Test Part Five

Section A

- Read the newspaper bulletin about a joint venture.
- In most lines **1 - 5** there is **one extra word** which does not fit in. One or two lines, however, are correct.
- If a line is correct, write **CORRECT**.
- If there is an extra word in the line, write the **extra word in CAPITAL LETTERS**.

Example

0	I	T							

00	C	O	R	R	E	C	T		

Roysten plans US joint venture

0   Roysten, the engineering group, it plans to launch a US joint venture with

00   HarvestTate to set up a factory to make up to 1,000 buses a year. The   ✓

1   agreement is one the first product of the strategic alliance with HarvestTate   *one*

2   that Roysten announced in May. Roysten's joint venture partner will be   ✓

3   Freerider, a HarvestTate subsidiary and leading manufacturer of school buses. ✓

4   The two parties are aiming to lease out or buy a factory capable of producing   *~~at~~ out*

5   1,000 buses a year, which selling at $150,000 each. Roysten's shares closed   *~~at~~ which*

     22p higher at 246p.

sort of rent

Writing Test Part One (i)

- You are the manager of a small office. In order to reduce costs and improve the company's environmental practices, you have decided to collect and recycle all paper used in the office.

- Write a memo of **30 - 40 words**:

  *   informing staff of the new policy
  *   explaining how the paper will be collected
  *   requesting staff to co-operate with the scheme.

Writing Test Part One (ii)

- You are the office manager at an insurance company. You have arranged for contractors to upgrade your computer system. This means the system will be shut down for a full day.

- Write a memo of **30 - 40 words**:

  *   informing staff of the shutdown
  *   telling them when it will happen
  *   asking them to prepare alternative work for the day.

Health and safety

Injuries at work

Speaking **1** Think of three accidents that can happen in an office.

Reading 1 **2** Look at the table showing the most common causes of office injuries in the UK. Complete the information with the percentages in the box.

15%	7%	35%	25%	12%

Office Injuries 1991-1997

In the UK, in the six-year period to 1997, there were 3,657 injuries to employees which resulted in them being absent from work for more than 3 days.

Table 1: Causes of over 3-day injuries in the office

..... resulted from being struck by a moving object.

..... resulted from a fall from a height.

..... resulted from handling, lifting or carrying an object.

..... resulted from the person striking a fixed object.

..... resulted from a slip or trip.

Now turn to page 147 to check your answers.

Speaking **3** How do these accidents happen? How could they be prevented?

4 An employee visits the company nurse after he has had an accident at work.
Listen and complete Part D of the accident report form below.

Health and Safety at Work etc Act 1974
The Reporting of Injuries, Diseases and Dangerous Occurrences Regulations 1995

Report of an injury or dangerous occurrence

Filling in this form
This form must be filled in by an employer or other responsible person.

Part A

About the injured person
Full name

Peter Gough

Home address

25 London Road
Canterbury

Job title

Export Document Supervisor

Part B

About the incident
Date and time of the incident

17/6/2000   2.15 pm

Place of the incident

Office 239

Part C

About the injury
Description of the injury

Small cut and
bump to head.

Part D

Description of the incident

The patient was in
his office trying to fix
(1) .... He
stood on his desk, but
lost (2) .... and
fell. He sustained a
small cut to his head
and a bump.
    I cleaned and
dressed the wound.
No (3) .... were
needed. The patient did
not feel sick or dizzy
but complained that he
was experiencing pain.
I gave him some
(4) .... and
told him to come
back the next day.

Grammar 5 Now look at the tapescript and underline all the verbs of obligation. Use the verbs to
complete the table below. Think of more words or phrases to add to each category.

Obligation	Negative obligation	Absence of obligation
must	mustn't	doesn't have to

Speaking 6 What health and safety obligations are there at your company?

How safe is your workplace?

Reading 2 ❶ Read the leaflet about risk assessment. Choose the best title for each of the five steps.

Step 1 .....

Step 2 .....

Step 3 .....

Step 4 .....

Step 5 .....

A	Decide who might be harmed
B	Look for the hazards
C	Revise your assessment
D	Record your findings
E	Evaluate the risks arising from the hazards

❷ Now choose the correct sentence from the opposite page to fill each gap. The first one is already done for you.

5 STEPS TO RISK ASSESSMENT ...

Risk assessment is nothing more than a careful examination of what, in your work, could cause harm to people, so that you can decide whether you have taken enough precautions or should do more to prevent harm. Its aim is to make sure that no one gets hurt or becomes ill. Accidents and ill health can ruin lives and affect your business too if output is lost, machinery is damaged, insurance costs increase, or you have to go to court.

The important things you need to decide in risk assessment are whether a hazard is significant and whether you have it covered by satisfactory precautions so that the risk is small.

If you are a small firm and you are confident you understand the work, you can do the assessment yourself. (0) ..I.. If you are not confident, ask your local Health and Safety Inspector to advise you. But remember: you are responsible for seeing that adequate precautions are taken.

Step 1 Walk around your workplace and look afresh at what could reasonably be expected to cause harm. Ignore the trivial and concentrate only on significant hazards which could result in serious harm or affect several people. **(1)** ..... Because they experience the workplace and work practices on a daily basis, they may have noticed things which are not immediately obvious.

Step 2 Think about people who may not be in the workplace all the time, e.g. cleaners, contractors, maintenance personnel. **(2)** ..... There is a chance that they could be hurt by your activities.

Step 3 Even after all precautions have been taken, usually some risk remains. What you have to decide for each significant hazard is whether this remaining risk is high, medium or low. First, ask yourself whether you have done all the things that the law says you have got to do. Then ask yourself whether generally accepted industry standards are in place. **(3)** ..... Remember: your aim is to make all risks small by adding to your precautions if necessary.

Step 4 If you have fewer than five employees, you do not need to write anything down, but if you have five or more employees, you must record the significant findings of your assessment. This means writing down the more significant hazards and recording your most important conclusions. You should keep the written document for future reference. It will be particularly useful if an inspector questions your precautions or if you become involved in an action for civil liability. **(4)** ..... And it can remind you to keep an eye on particular matters or causes for concern.

Step 5 At some time, you will undoubtedly bring in new machines, substances and procedures which could lead to new hazards. **(5)** ..... In any case, it is good practice to review your assessment from time to time. Don't amend your assessment for every trivial change or each new job; but if a new job introduces significant new hazards of its own, you will want to consider them in their own right and do whatever you need to keep the risks down.

Adapted from 5 Steps to Risk Assessment, Health and Safety Executive

A   It also helps to show that you have done what the law requires.

B   Improving health and safety need not cost a lot.

C   Where such hazards are unavoidable, use appropriate safety equipment.

D   But don't stop there - think for yourself, because the law also says that you must do what is reasonable to keep your workplace safe.

E   If there is any significant change, you should take this into account.

F   Members of the public who visit your workplace should also be included.

G   Ask your employees or their representatives what they think.

H   For instance, electricity can kill, but in an office environment the risk is remote.

I   Alternatively, you could ask a responsible employee, safety representative or safety officer to help you.

What helped you to choose your answers?

Speaking ❸   Work in pairs. Find out about the following features at your partner's workplace. Give each feature a mark out of 5. Add up the total score out of 40.

Working Environment Survey

Are you happy with your working environment?

Your Health & Safety Representatives will be meeting next week to discuss recommendations to improve the working environment within the company. Please help us by completing this questionnaire.

	😟 1	2	😐 3	4	🙂 5
Safety equipment	☐	☐	☐	☐	☐
First aid facilities	☐	☐	☐	☐	☐
Ventilation	☐	☐	☐	☐	☐
Lighting	☐	☐	☐	☐	☐
Temperature	☐	☐	☐	☐	☐
Individual work space	☐	☐	☐	☐	☐
Drinking water	☐	☐	☐	☐	☐
Washroom facilities	☐	☐	☐	☐	☐

Please return your completed questionnaire to Paul Sykes (Ext.312).

How could you improve the three worst features?

Rights at work

Know your rights

Speaking ❶ Discuss the following questions about smoking in the workplace.

- Should employees have an automatic right to smoke at work?
- Should employers be allowed to ask smokers who take frequent smoking breaks to work extra hours?
- How can employers balance the interests of smokers and non-smokers?
- What should employers do if they cannot meet the needs of both smokers and non-smokers?

Reading ❷ Read the bulletin on the opposite page about an industrial tribunal on smoking. Who won the case - the plaintiff or the employer? How will this decision affect employers in the future?

❸ Read the bulletin again. Are the following statements true or false?

1 The plaintiff was asked to leave the company.
2 The plaintiff was the only person disturbed by the smoke.
3 The company formulated a smoking policy.
4 The company was obliged by law to deal with staff complaints.
5 All employers who ban smoking will face claims for unfair dismissal.

Tribunal rules on smoking at work case

Beware this cloudy issue, warns employment law specialist

EMPLOYERS must take sufficient steps to protect non-smoking employees from tobacco smoke or they might be faced with legal action, warns law firm Thomas, Snell & Passmore.

Jill Thomas, an employment law specialist with the firm, quotes a recent case brought before the Employment Appeal Tribunal (EAT).

An employer's failure to protect its employees against tobacco smoke caused an employee to quit her job. Whilst working, the employee was forced to work near four secretaries who smoked and the rooms of three solicitors who smoked cigarettes, cigars and a pipe. All doors were kept open to allow ventilation from the smoking rooms.

After a series of complaints from the plaintiff and fellow colleagues, the employer consulted staff and agreed that a smoking policy should be drawn up. However, the policy did not go far enough to solve the problem for the plaintiff. She was finally told either to put up with the smoke or leave, which she did.

The EAT ruled that the employer had breached its contractual obligation to deal reasonably and promptly with its employees' grievances, and to provide a reasonable working environment suitable for its employees. The plaintiff was awarded damages.

But employers are advised to think carefully before they rush into implementing or enforcing smoking bans. Unless they take care, they could be faced with unfair dismissal claims from smokers - precisely what they were trying to avoid with non-smokers.

Before introducing a total or partial smoking ban, employers are recommended to protect themselves from potential claims by smokers. Staff must be consulted on their views and given reasonable notice of any changes. Employers should then sensibly enforce their smoking ban.

Adapted from the *Company Digest* website: www.companydigest.co.uk

Company Digest

28

Speaking **4** Do you think the decision of the EAT was fair? Why/Why not?

Grammar **5** Read the bulletin again and underline examples of passive forms. Which of them go in the following groups?

Obligation	Recommendation	Possibility
staff must be consulted	a smoking policy should be drawn up	they might be faced with ...

Writing **6** Formulate a smoking policy for your office which is fair to both smokers and non-smokers. Write a 30-40 word memo informing all staff of the policy.

Problems at work

Listening **1** Five people talk about why they lost their jobs. Listen and decide the reason each speaker gives.

1 .....

2 .....

3 .....

4 .....

5 .....

A failure to meet targets
B personal use of company property
C poor time keeping
D refusal to observe safety regulations
E refusal to commute
F refusal to work overtime
G repeated absence from work
H sexual harassment

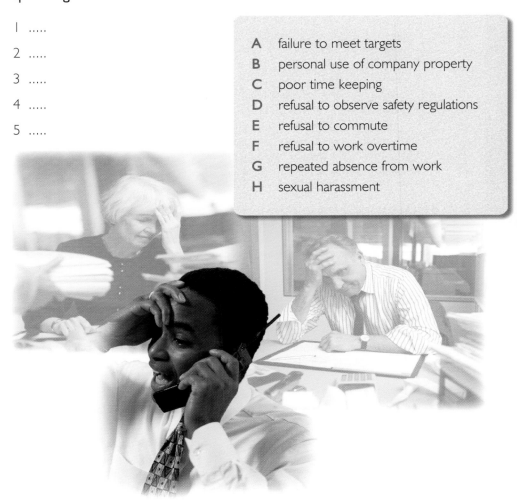

Speaking **2** Do you think any of the speakers were treated unfairly?

Speaking **3** Work in pairs. As a manager, how would you deal with the incidents below? Would you:

- take no action against the person?
- have a friendly word with the person?
- give an official verbal warning?
- give an official written warning?
- dismiss the person?

1 An employee who repeatedly refuses to observe safety requirements has caused a small fire. Little damage has been caused and no-one has been hurt.

2 You hear that an employee has physically threatened a colleague. This is the first time he has behaved this way.

3 An employee has told a friend (a journalist) about secret negotiations your company is having about the takeover of another company. The story appears on the front page of a national newspaper.

4 An employee has come to work and is acting strangely. You talk to her and can smell alcohol on her breath.

5 You discover that information a new employee has included on her curriculum vitae is not true. She has exaggerated her experience and lied about her qualifications.

6 A new member of the secretarial staff arrives a few minutes late and leaves a few minutes early every day. Also, she takes fifteen minutes or more extra at lunchtime. Several of her colleagues have been heard to complain about this.

7 As you are leaving the office, you notice an employee putting a packet of photocopier paper in his bag.

8 An employee, frustrated with his computer, has hit it violently. The machine is irreparable and a replacement will cost £1,200.

1 **Choose the correct word to complete each sentence.**

1   It is important to assess any new hazards which (*rise/arise*) in the workplace.

2   Health and safety measures are designed to (*prevent/protect*) employees.

3   You can seriously injure your back if you try to (*handle/lift*) a heavy object.

4   The cleaners had just washed the floor in the washroom, and I (*slipped/tripped*) on it.

5   We hope to avoid any further (*accidents/incidents*) of theft.

6   He wasn't seriously (*wounded/injured*). It was just a small cut.

7   Could I see the nurse? I've fallen and (*harmed/hurt*) my back.

8   You must take all reasonable (*precautions/predictions*) against accidents.

9   You are (*enquired/required*) to keep a record of all significant hazards.

10 Please consider the risks faced by maintenance (*personnel/personal*).

2 **Complete each sentence with the correct form of the word in capital letters.**

1   HARM
None of the substances we use here are _____ , so there's no danger.

2   INJURE
How did the _____ happen?

3   OBLIGE
Employers have a legal _____ to protect staff.

4   FIND
Only the significant _____ of your assessment need to be written down.

5   HAZARD
You need to take extra care when handling _____ materials.

6   SAFE
Health and _____ representatives will be meeting next week.

7   LIABLE
Keep a record of all accidents in case you become involved in a civil _____ action.

3 **Complete each sentence with a suitable preposition.**

1   The lights keep going _____ . We'll have to get maintenance to fix them.

2   The risk _____ an accident happening is remote.

3   Their first aid facilities are cause _____ concern.

4   The written document will be useful _____ future reference.

5   Concentrate _____ the most significant hazards.

6   You should take _____ account members of the public who might visit your workplace.

7   These accidents resulted in two company cleaners being absent _____ work for two days.

8   How can such incidents be prevented _____ happening again?

Modal verbs

4 **Choose the correct verb to complete each sentence.**

1   You (*needn't/mustn't*) amend your assessment for every trivial change - only the most significant ones.

2   Even after all precautions have been taken, some risks (*could/should*) still remain.

3   (*Shall/Will*) I fill in the accident report form?

4   Not all hazards (*must/can*) be avoided.

5   NB: Employees (*must not/cannot*) lift heavy objects without proper training.

6   If you're not too busy, (*will/shall*) you help me put up these safety notices?

7   If the employer is found responsible for an accident, he (*could/is able to*) be in trouble.

8   (*May/Will*) I use your phone to make a quick call?

9   I don't think they'll find anything wrong with the ventilation system, but, of course, they (*might/can*).

10 I (*don't need to/mustn't*) see the nurse. It isn't a very serious injury.

11 This first aid box is very old. Do you think we (*should/would*) get a new one?

12 When you are assessing risks, you (*could/would*) ask a responsible employee to help you.

Complete the sentences with the following verbs.

put up with	keep up with	meet
prioritise	draw up	deal with

1 We try to _____ all complaints reasonably.

2 My employers agreed to _____ a smoking policy.

3 The woman _____ the smoke for a long time before making a formal complaint.

4 Employers must try to _____ the needs of all their employees.

5 He tried to _____ the ever-increasing workload, but it was too much for him.

6 If you are very busy, it is important to _____ all the things to be done.

Read through the unit and the tapescript. Find more words and phrases connected with the law.

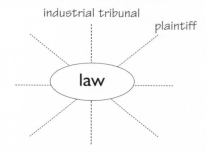

industrial tribunal

plaintiff

law

Choose the correct word to complete each sentence.

1 If an employee has a (grievance/failure), the company should deal with it promptly and fairly.

2 I refused to (rest/stay) late at work every day.

3 We lost the case but it was no-one's (guilt/fault).

4 Employees must (observe/watch) safety regulations.

5 He caused a lot of (damage/hurt) to his computer.

6 If you ban smoking at work, some people will (complain/threaten).

7 Some smokers take (frequent/often) breaks.

8 He failed to (hit/meet) his monthly sales targets.

9 She complained that smoking in the office (disturbed/minded) her and made her feel ill.

10 Should we have an automatic (claim/right) to smoke at work?

4 Complete the table.

Verb	Noun
exaggerate	....
justify	....
abuse	....
ban	....
behave	....
negotiate	....
refuse	....
complain	....

5 Put these in order from the least to the most serious.

A His boss gave him an official verbal warning.
B His boss dismissed him.
C His boss took no action against him.
D His boss gave him an official written warning.
E His boss had a friendly word with him.

Passives

6 Change sentences A-D from Exercise 5 into the passive.

A   *He was given an official verbal warning.*
B   _____
C   _____
D   _____

7 Complete this conversation with the correct passive form of the verbs in brackets.

● What's happened to Dave Wright from Accounts?

▼ Haven't you heard? He (1 sack)   *'s been sacked* .

● He's lost his job? But why? How?

▼ Well, when the company (2 take over) _____ last June, he was told he'd have to relocate. He refused and he (3 just/tell) _____ to go.

● That's terrible! Poor Dave! What do you think he'll do?

▼ Well, actually, he's not so upset. He's been applying for some other jobs and he's sure that he (4 offer) _____ a job by Elite Finance.

● Do you think he'll take it?

▼ I'm sure he will - if he (5 offer) _____ enough money.

● And has anybody else (6 tell) _____ to leave?

▼ I'm not sure. Let's wait and see.

Reading Test Part Three

- Read the text below about a department store group and answer questions **1 - 8**.

Horners Department Stores

Horners operates from 32 department stores in the UK, which are situated either in prime High Street locations or out of town retail parks. Specialising in the clothing, accessories, and home product markets, Horners has become one of the country's favourite department stores and offers a range of high quality, competitively-priced merchandise to its customers.

1 Over recent years there has been a steady decline in the number of UK department stores which do not belong to a chain. On the other hand, the top three national department store groups account for an increasing proportion of the department store market. This clearly reflects their ability to make a success of this retailing format in the UK. Horners is a market leader within this group, differentiating itself from its main competitors as a large space clothing-led retailer offering its own, as well as international brands.

2 The creation of an attractive and appealing selling environment is one of the most important aspects of successful retailing. Horners has devoted a significant amount of management time to providing a relaxing, highly visual and efficient environment which makes shopping in a Horners store a pleasure. Exciting and creative merchandise displays provide each section with a clearly distinguishable look, and these are frequently updated in all stores. These are supported by point of sale displays to emphasise product quality and to increase appeal. The attraction of the stores is further reinforced by easy access for customers throughout the store.

3 Department stores appeal to people of all age groups, but particularly the 30 - 50 age category. Consumers here are generally in the higher income groups and are more demanding in terms of the quality of service they expect. This age group is expected to account for an increasing proportion of the overall population over the next decade. By the year 2001, this age group is projected to grow by just over 8 per cent, compared to the total population, which is projected to grow by only 1.6 per cent.

4 We aim to give our customers the widest possible product choice, and we have been highly successful in developing our own brands, which now account for almost 50 per cent of sales. Horners also has exclusive relationships with a number of leading designers, who design clothing, accessories and home product ranges to suit our customer profile. Supported by strong visual presentation, these exclusive ranges have attracted new customers into the stores through extensive television, newspaper and magazine publicity campaigns. To maximise the profit generated by each store, Horners constantly monitors and adjusts the allocation of retail space dedicated to each of these product categories.

Questions 1 - 4

- For questions **1 - 4**, choose the best title for each numbered paragraph from the box below.
- For each numbered paragraph **1 - 4**, mark **one** letter **A - G**.
- Do not use any letter more than once.

A	Customer profile
B	Public relations
C	Store layout and design
D	Customer services
E	Store location
F	Merchandise
G	Market climate

1 Paragraph 1 .....

2 Paragraph 2 .....

3 Paragraph 3 .....

4 Paragraph 4 .....

Questions 5 - 8

- Using the information in the text, complete each sentence with a phrase **A - G** from the list below.
- For each question **5 - 8**, mark one letter **A - G**.
- Do not use any letter more than once.

5   Independent department stores have found it difficult to .....

6   Horners realises the need to regularly .....

7   Typical Horners' customers generally .....

8   Horners contracts leading designers to .....

A	emphasise the need for low prices.
B	develop own-label products.
C	appeal to customers of all ages.
D	compete in this retail sector.
E	provide a relaxed atmosphere.
F	modernise in-store displays.
G	expect a high standard of service.

Reading Test Part Five Section B

- Read the text below from a brochure about a transport company.
- In each line there is **one wrong word**.
- For each line **1 - 5**, write the **correct word in CAPITAL LETTERS**.

Example

0 | A | | | | | | | |

00 | A | T | | | | | | |

0   Delivering the load is only part of our whole operation. An comprehensive and

00 efficient administration service is also essential for operating in the high

1   standards demanded from today's customers. Centrally controlled, our group

2   administration department is a channel for each information about each and

3   every delivery. That department is responsible for giving our customers a wide

4   range of information, what involves processing proof of delivery documents,

5   provide delivery updates with our unique tracking system and full pallet control.

Writing Paper Part One

- You are the Head of Personnel at a large international company. You have just appointed Ms Francesca Bianchi as the new Sales Manager at Head Office.

- Write a memo of **30 - 40 words** to Head Office staff:

  * announcing Ms Bianchi's appointment
  * saying when she will start work
  * asking staff to give her a friendly welcome.

Business expenses

Claiming expenses

Speaking ❶ **What expenses do people typically incur on a business trip?**

❷ **What would you do in the following situations?**

Situation One

On a three-day business trip to Paris, yo travel around the city using the undergroun system to visit clients. You find this th cheapest and most convenient way c travelling. On your last night there, you begi filling in your expenses claim sheet. When yo read the small print, you notice you ar authorised to claim up to £25 per day for taxi:

Situation Two

Your first business trip for your new company has been successful and you have secured an important new contract. You invite your client out to dinner at an expensive restaurant. However, at the end of the meal, he insists on paying the bill. It comes to £125. He passes you the receipt after he has paid and says you could claim this back on expenses. 'Everyone does it,' he says.

Situation Three

You discover that a colleague has made a fals claim for expenses for a five-day trip t Hamburg. He was booked into a hotel whic cost £80 per night, but he only stayed there fc one night. He then checked out of the hote and spent the rest of the week with an o friend. However, he made an expenses clair for all five nights.

Listening 1 ❸ Roger Hargreaves works in an accounts department. He telephones three people about their expenses claims. Listen and complete the forms below with one or two words or a number.

Sofrac Limited

Expenses Claim Form - Management   Name: David Hobbs   Date: 16·7

Full details (inc date)	Accommodation	Business Travel	Client Entertaining	Other Expenses	Total
July 3·99 Business Trip (1)	Cartlands Hotel One night (2)	Train 1st class return £84	Meal/Drinks (3) £56·70	(4) £9	

Telephone Message

To: Alan Hayworth
Date: 30·7·99

Taken by: Alison
Time: 3·30 pm

Roger Hargreaves from Accounts called about expenses for your trip to (5) _____ last month.

He hasn't got the (6) _____. He needs this asap. If you can't find it, you should (7) _____

He's sorry but Accounts can't make (8) _____ like last time.

Sof~~rac Limited~~

Expenses Claim Form - Management   Name: Chris Evans   Date: 24·7·99

Full details (inc date)	Accommodation	Business Travel	Client Entertaining	Other Expenses	Total
Two-day recruitment trip to Paris (9) June	One night (10)	(11)	N/A	(12) £5	

Speaking ❹ Explain the system for claiming expenses in your company. How could it be improved?

Business expenses   Unit 8a   108

A new expenses claims system

Reading **1** Read the memo below about a new expenses claims system. Answer the questions.

1 What are the two main components of the new system?
2 How will the new system save the company money?
3 Who will be e-mailed an electronic form each month?
4 Which expenses will be shown on the e-mailed form?
5 What additional information will the claimant be required to give?
6 How will the company check that employees are not abusing the system?

MEMO

TO: All Heads of Department

FROM: Alan Lock, Accounts Manager

SUBJECT: IMPLEMENTATION OF NEW EXPENSES SYSTEM

As you know, this department has undertaken an extensive survey into alternative systems of handling corporate travel expenses and expenses claims. In recent months, a corporate charge card (Amex) and an automated expenses reimbursement system have been trialled successfully in several departments. This system will now be implemented throughout the organisation. The main benefits of the new system are that cash advances will no longer be necessary and administrative time can be reduced. It will also cut the cost of processing each claim and should produce a substantial saving on the time employees spend on claiming expenses. The system should be fully operational within the next ten weeks. A brief outline of how the system works is given below.

CLAIMING EXPENSES

Employees who travel on company business will be sent a form by e-mail each month that shows all purchases made on their Amex card. Employees indicate the business purpose of each purchase and, in the case of entertainment expenses, give the names of guests. Employees deduct personal expenses incurred on the card and add corporate expenses paid for in cash. The company will then settle up with one monthly cheque to Amex for all the business expenses incurred using the card. It will then be the employee's responsibility to settle the balance for personal expenses.

AUDITING PROCEDURES

Line managers will monitor expenses claims, making a random check of between 15 and 20 per cent of all claims submitted.

Full details of the new system will be sent to all Heads of Department within the next few days.

Speaking **2** Discuss the advantages and disadvantages of this system.

Listening 2 **3** Five people call the Accounts Department and leave messages about their
expenses. Listen and decide what each speaker is trying to do.

1 .....

2 .....

3 .....

4 .....

5 .....

A	arrange a meeting
B	ask for help
C	ask for information
D	ask permission
E	cancel an appointment
F	explain a delay
G	make a complaint
H	thank someone

Speaking **4** Why might people experience the following feelings when claiming expenses?

guilt	frustration	surprise
disappointment	relief	worry

Writing **5** You work in the Accounts Department and are responsible for checking employees'
expenses. Write a 30-40 word memo to staff:

- reminding them of the importance of receipts
- telling them how expenses will be paid
- saying how long expenses payments take to process.

Business travel

Airline services

Speaking **Work in groups. Look at this list of airline services. Agree on the three most important services for the business traveller.**

- air-miles awards for frequent flyers

- valet service airport parking

- double baggage allowance

- priority status at check-in

- exclusive business lounges

- advanced seat selection

- wider, fully reclining seats

- in-seat phone/fax facilities

- in-flight catering/free drinks

Listening ❷ Five business travellers talk about different air travel services. Decide which one each speaker is talking about.

1	A	business class section
2	B	comfortable seating
3	C	free newspapers and magazines
4	D	in-flight entertainment
5	E	in-flight food and drink
	F	in-seat phone/fax facilities
	G	on-board duty-free sales
	H	scheduled flights

Speaking ❸ Work in pairs. Find out about three airlines your partner has flown with. Which offered the best service and why?

No frills flying

Speaking ❶ What differences are there between mainstream airlines and low-cost airlines?

Reading 1 ❷ Read the article on the following page. What examples of mainstream and low-cost airlines are mentioned? Which airline is the cheapest?

October 1998

Flying high with cheap frills

Low-cost airlines are offering deals to woo business travellers, writes Gillian Upton

1 When is a low-cost airline not a 'no-frills' airline? When it adds frills. Business travellers who have taken enthusiastically to value-for-money air travel are now being offered packages more commonly associated with mainstream airlines.

2 To date, the attraction of no-frills airlines has been based on price; forget the more convenient departure points, creature comforts or ease of scheduling. Easyjet, Ryanair and Debonair have all undercut leading carriers by as much as 70 per cent on high volume routes.

3 However, in the wake of increased competition and aggressive price-cutting from mainstream airlines such as KLM UK, three no-frills airlines are changing tack. Virgin Express is increasing legroom and is contemplating the launch of a frequent-flyer programme; Go, owned by British Airways, is wooing the business traveller; and

Debonair is introducing a business class section next week.

4 Debonair, based at Luton Airport, north of London, was launched just over two years ago and went into profit for the first time this summer. Even when it started, it set itself

slightly apart from its low-cost competitors by offering more seat comfort, a drink in-flight and a simple frequent-flyer scheme.

5 Debonair's business class, called ABC, will give passengers more privacy during the flight, a fully-refundable, flexible ticket, a free bar, a snack and a dedicated check-in desk. Yet the fare will remain as much as 40 per cent below the average business class ticket price.

6 Other low-cost airlines, however, are standing firm. Even so, Easyjet, which markets itself on lowest price, no catering and direct sell, has now introduced a £10 charge to allow its passengers to transfer from one Easyjet flight to another. This is effectively a concession to the business traveller, who needs more flexibility.

7 Attempts by Virgin Express, Go and Debonair to move upmarket are being viewed by some as the beginning of a consolidation in the sector. With so much competition on price, it seems likely that some players in the low-cost airline business will fail to survive.

13

---

3 Read the article again. Think of a title for each paragraph.

4 Read the article again. Are the following statements true or false?

1 The differences between mainstream and low-cost airlines are becoming less clear.
2 Low-cost airlines are only slightly cheaper than mainstream airlines.
3 Mainstream airlines are offering extra services to compete with low-cost airlines.
4 Debonair offers more services to passengers than other low-cost airlines.
5 Easyjet is refusing to change its approach in any way for business travellers.
6 The number of low-cost airlines is set to grow in the future.

Speaking **5** How do you see the future for mainstream and low-cost airlines?

6 **Look at the comments below from passengers who flew with low-cost airlines. Which airline does each of the following sentences refer to?**

1 This airline provided the best service.
2 This airline provided the worst service.
3 This airline offered no in-flight food for its passengers.
4 This airline offered the best value in terms of in-flight catering.
5 The check-in procedures for this airline were confused.
6 The check-in procedures for this airline were highly efficient.
7 The interior of this airline's plane was dirty.

Sophie Little, a passenger with *Fastjet*
The check-in person told me to collect my ticket at the ticket desk. But there, they told me I didn't need one and sent me back to check-in. On the plane itself I was surprised to get lunch and a free drink. I didn't think that usually happened with low-cost airlines. It was very nice, but it didn't make up for the fact that we left an hour late.

Marion Palmer, a passenger with *Swiftair*
Incredibly, from check-in desk to my seat took less than twenty minutes. My seat was a little uncomfortable, but the fact that there were no delays made this bearable, as did a nice cup of real coffee and a tasty cheese sandwich, both reasonably priced.

Johnathan Ives, a passenger with *Prestige*
They announced there would be a delay on the flight - but didn't give a reason for it. On board, duty-free goods were available, but the same couldn't be said about any form of refreshment. Luckily, I'd had a big breakfast at the airport.

Simon Stevens, a passenger with *World Air*
Checking in took forever, as did take-off. Inside, the level of comfort and standard of cleanliness were extremely disappointing, and there weren't enough sandwiches for all the passengers, so most went hungry. I was one of the unlucky ones who got one!

Speaking **7** **Work in pairs. Tell your partner about your best and worst experiences of air travel.**

1 Complete the telephone conversation with questions.

▼ Hello. This is David Bridge from Accounts. I'm just ringing about your expenses claim for your Paris trip. You only wrote down the total figure you spent - but I need more information.

● Oh, sorry. What do you need to know?

▼ Well, first of all, (1) _____ ?

● Let me see. Yes. It was the 1st and 2nd of June.

▼ Right. And (2) _____ ?

● It was a sales conference I was attending.

▼ I see. And (3) _____ Paris?

● By plane. I flew from Gatwick.

▼ OK. Now (4) _____ ?

● At the Hotel Deluxe.

▼ Right. And (5) _____ ?

● Just one night. I flew back on the 2nd.

▼ OK. And (6) _____ ?

● Dupont. Pascale Dupont.

▼ (7) _____ ?

● Dupont? Yes, it's D-U-P-O-N-T.

▼ Thanks. And now could you just send me the receipts?

2 Match the words.

1	false	manager
2	random	claim
3	small	check
4	line	print
5	short	notice

Now use the combinations to complete the sentences.

1 All expenses claims sheets must be authorised by your _____ .

2 He had to leave at _____ and had no time to update me.

3 To stop people abusing the system, we will make a _____ of 10 % of all claims.

4 The new automated system should help us catch anyone trying to make a _____ .

5 If you read the _____ , you'll see that we do not accept liability for any loss or damage.

3 Read through the unit. Find verbs which occur before these nouns.

_____to claim_____

_____ expenses

_____

_____

_____ an expenses claim

_____

4 Complete the table.

Verb	Noun
supply	....
reimburse	....
claim	....
authorise	....
require	....
automate	....

Relative pronouns

5 Correct any mistakes with the relative pronouns in the note below. Can any of the pronouns be omitted?

Dear Mr Rivers

I enclose the expenses claim form who you sent to me last week as it is incomplete. I need to know the names of the clients that you took for lunch and the name of the restaurant where you took them to. I also need to know the reason for the £25 what you put in the last column. Please also note that it is only line managers whom can authorise expenses, not colleagues whose work in your office.

Kind regards

6 Join each pair of sentences using a relative pronoun.

1 I took Mr Fuller to lunch. He is a client.

2 Employees travel on company business. They will be sent a form by e-mail each month.

3 The expenses claims system will be implemented next month. It will cut costs considerably.

4 I received the expenses claims form. You sent it to me on 27 November.

5 Those are the employees. We paid their expenses last week.

Match the words.

1	duty	flight
2	baggage	free
3	check-in	allowance
4	scheduled	desk
5	in-flight	catering
6	reclining	status
7	priority	seat

Change the following words into adjectives. Put them into the correct group below.

reason	exclude	bear	annoy
disappoint	compete		refund
entertain	transfer	recline	select

- able	- ing	- ive
reasonable		

Put these actions into a logical order.

A Our flight was called.
B We checked in.
C We took off.
D We landed in Paris an hour later.
E We waited in the departure lounge.
F We went through passport control and customs.
G On board we bought some duty-free cigarettes.
H We went to the ticket desk to collect our tickets.
I We boarded the plane.

Complete each sentence with a suitable preposition.

1 The free meal didn't make up _____ the delay.

2 Their attraction is based _____ price.

3 No reason _____ the long delay was given.

4 The in-flight meal was good value _____ money.

5 Debonair is based _____ Luton airport.

6 These times don't fit in _____ your plans.

7 Fastjet provides the best value _____ terms
   _____ in-flight catering.

8 _____ the wake of increased competition, certain
   airlines are changing strategy.

⑤ Complete the sentences with the following verbs.

undercut	raise	survive
transfer	compete	fail

1 Aggressive price-cutting means some no-frills airlines
   may not _____ .

2 Several mainstream airlines _____ on
   price with low-cost carriers.

3 Normally, if you buy the cheapest ticket, you can't
   _____ to another flight.

4 We don't intend to _____ ticket
   prices. We intend to lower them.

5 Their prices _____ other airlines by as
   much as 70% on high volume routes.

6 Certain airlines may _____ to attract
   customers if they maintain such high prices.

Indirect questions

⑥ Re-arrange the words to make indirect questions.

1 you where could check me in tell we
   Could you tell me where we check in?

2 when know 'd to off like I take we
   _____

3 refundable just can this if I ticket ask is
   _____

4 is tell could why delay a there me you
   _____

5 tell if meal could board you me get on we a
   _____

⑦ Make these questions more polite.

1 Is there any in-flight entertainment?
   _____

2 Do you offer a frequent flyer programme?
   _____

3 Where's the business lounge?
   _____

4 What time do we leave?
   _____

5 Are the seats reclining?
   _____

6 Where can I exchange money?
   _____

Reading Test Part Four

- Read the text below about flexible working.
- Choose the correct word from **A**, **B**, **C** or **D** to fill each gap.
- For each gap **I - 15**, mark **one** letter **A**, **B**, **C** or **D**.

Flexible working

The term 'flexible working' has become familiar to any company, regardless of size, that needs to look at how **(0)** ..... jobs are structured. The thinking behind this is not only the realisation that this **(1)** ..... has potential cost benefits, but also the recognition that it can lead to a more **(2)** ..... and contented workforce.

One company with a long **(3)** ..... of flexible working is Remploy, the UK's largest employer of severely **(4)** ..... people. Remploy has a UK workforce of more than 11,000 **(5)** ..... in 89 factories working in various **(6)** ..... of the economy including textiles, furniture and manufacturing services.

Training and development **(7)** ..... are a key aspect of Remploy's employment policy, and each hourly-paid employee has an individual training and action **(8)** ..... . Throughout the company, there is also an awareness that progression, and the opportunity to progress, is a **(9)** ..... factor. In the Manufacturing Services Group, for example, the policy is to **(10)** ..... as many employees as possible in two of the core businesses. Once they have achieved this, the employees are **(11)** ..... .

In addition, Remploy has **(12)** ..... to changing markets in recent years by changing products in over a third of its factories. This has enabled the company to **(13)** ..... competitive and keep the workforce in full-time **(14)** ..... . On these occasions, Remploy's flexible approach has enabled employees to be fully retrained whilst **(15)** ..... to work.

Example

0	A individual	B sole	C single	D unique

A B C D
▬ ▭ ▭ ▭

I	A course	B manner	C approach	D technique
2	A fruitful	B inventive	C beneficial	D productive
3	A history	B story	C report	D account
4	A disabled	B weak	C sick	D injured
5	A employees	B colleagues	C subordinates	D workmates
6	A pieces	B divisions	C quarters	D sectors
7	A agendas	B lists	C programmes	D tables
8	A project	B plan	C system	D procedure
9	A prompting	B motivating	C persuading	D moving
10	A train	B improve	C guide	D learn
II	A raised	B supported	C promoted	D developed
12	A replied	B answered	C returned	D responded
13	A remain	B continue	C rest	D stand
14	A use	B engagement	C exercise	D employment
15	A maintaining	B staying	C continuing	D lasting

Writing Test Part Two

- You are the manager of an office supplies company. A colleague has received a letter complaining about an order for office furniture. She has left the letter for you to answer and has written some notes on it.
- Write a **100 - 120 word** reply using the letter below and the handwritten notes.
- Do not include addresses.

Bureautech
33 avenue Louis Blanc
75019 Paris
France

The Manager
Adhoc Designs
29 George Street
Dover
England

June 28 1999

Order No. B13 / 4620

Dear Sir

> Apologise.

I am writing to complain about your handling of the above order for 20 Linsdon office desks and to say how disappointed we are with how this order has been dealt with.

> Explain why.

When we placed our order with you in April, we were assured that the desks would be sent to us within four weeks. In fact, it has actually taken nearly two months to deliver the goods.

> Send next week.

In addition, two of the desks are badly damaged and will need replacing.

Also, we were told that as we were established customers, you would give us a special discount of 10 per cent off your catalogue prices. I note from your invoice that this discount has not been given.

I trust any future orders we place with you will be dealt with in a more satisfactory manner.

I look forward to your reply.

Yours faithfully

> Assure him of this.

> He's right. Send correct invoice & offer extra discount.

Paul Chandler
Manager

Flexible benefits

Benefits

Speaking ❶ Work in pairs. What benefits does your partner's company offer?

Reading 1 ❷ PricewaterhouseCoopers, the global professional services firm, operates a flexible benefits system called *Choices*. Which of the following might the employees below be interested in?

additional holiday	additional cash	retail vouchers
childcare vouchers	accident insurance	travel insurance
company car	pension	critical illness insurance

Julie is in her thirties and has a baby daughter. She has plans to return to work as soon as her daughter is old enough to go into day care.

Mark has joined PricewaterhouseCoopers after graduating from university. He is single and enjoys travelling. He would like to travel around the world with his girlfriend, who is still a student.

Susie and her partner both work full-time in well-paid jobs. Since they have no children, security is not a high priority. They are more concerned with enjoying life.

Speaking ❸ Imagine your company introduced a flexible benefits package. What benefits would you choose?

Reading 2 **1** Look at the information from a PricewaterhouseCoopers booklet about the firm's flexible benefits system. How are the Base Pay and Benefit Premium flexible?

How *Choices* works

The way your pay and benefits are put together under *Choices* is easy to understand:

Fig 1. *Your Total Reward is the sum of your Base Pay and Benefit Premium.*

Fig 2. *Your Benefit Premium is made up of Core Benefits and Additional Benefit Funding.*

Fig 3. *The flexible part of your Total Reward.*

Total Reward
Your Total Reward is made up of two elements - cash and benefits (Fig 1). *Choices* enables you to have a mix of Total Reward which suits you. To know how much can be spent on benefits, you start with Base Pay. Using this and other information (such as your grade and age) the Benefit Premium is calculated.

Benefit Premium
Your Benefit Premium is the additional amount over and above Base Pay which is provided to help fund your benefits. Your Benefit Premium is made up of two elements - Core Benefits and Additional Benefit Funding (Fig 2).

Core Benefits
As part of *Choices*, you are provided with certain minimum benefits which are funded by the firm and are not optional. These core benefits include a minimum number of days' holiday, life assurance and accident insurance.

In addition, for staff with longer service or at a certain level, a minimum amount of permanent health insurance and medical insurance is provided.

Additional Benefit Funding
You will be able to use as much as you like of your Additional Benefit Funding to 'buy' benefits. If you want more benefits than this can provide, you can also use up to 20% of your Base Pay. If you choose not to use all of your Additional Benefit Funding for benefits, you will be paid the balance in cash, as part of your monthly pay.

Your Additional Benefit Funding plus 20% of your Base Pay is the flexible part of your Total Reward (Fig 3).

2 Are the following statements true or false?

1 The amount of Benefit Premium varies according to the level of Base Pay.
2 The employee has to pay for all of the benefits offered by the firm.
3 Employees can have cash rather than life assurance.
4 All employees receive medical insurance.
5 Employees can have part of their Benefit Premium paid in cash.
6 The Additional Benefit Funding is equal to 20% of Base Pay.

Speaking **3** How important are benefits to you when considering a job offer?

The advantages of flexible benefits

Reading 3 ❶ Look at the information about the advantages of *Choices*. Complete the document with the correct benefit from the list below.

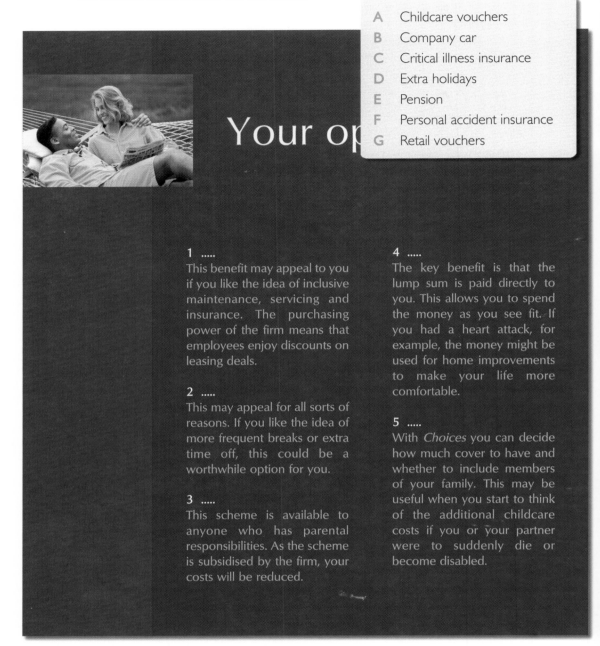

A Childcare vouchers
B Company car
C Critical illness insurance
D Extra holidays
E Pension
F Personal accident insurance
G Retail vouchers

Your op

1 .....
This benefit may appeal to you if you like the idea of inclusive maintenance, servicing and insurance. The purchasing power of the firm means that employees enjoy discounts on leasing deals.

2 .....
This may appeal for all sorts of reasons. If you like the idea of more frequent breaks or extra time off, this could be a worthwhile option for you.

3 .....
This scheme is available to anyone who has parental responsibilities. As the scheme is subsidised by the firm, your costs will be reduced.

4 .....
The key benefit is that the lump sum is paid directly to you. This allows you to spend the money as you see fit. If you had a heart attack, for example, the money might be used for home improvements to make your life more comfortable.

5 .....
With *Choices* you can decide how much cover to have and whether to include members of your family. This may be useful when you start to think of the additional childcare costs if you or your partner were to suddenly die or become disabled.

Listening ❷ David Thompson, a Senior Manager at PricewaterhouseCoopers, talks about the *Choices* scheme. Listen and choose one letter for the correct answer.

David Thompson
PricewaterhouseCoopers

1 PricewaterhouseCoopers launched *Choices* in order to
  A cater for the different needs of its employees.
  B reduce the cost of the company wage bill.
  C keep employees happy after the merger.

2 PricewaterhouseCoopers can offer benefits more cheaply because
  A it deals with cut-price providers.
  B all its benefits are tax-free.
  C of its bargaining power.

Flexible benefits

3 The purpose of the roadshows was to
   A distribute the printed information across the country.
   B give employees a chance to ask about *Choices*.
   C stop employees worrying about the merger.

4 In what way were the roadshows successful?
   A They allowed employees to choose their benefits.
   B They were attended by the majority of UK employees.
   C They increased awareness of the *Choices* scheme.

5 PricewaterhouseCoopers encouraged participation by
   A providing further details on its computer network.
   B sending detailed information to all employees.
   C telephoning all employees with more information.

6 David Thompson expects the most popular benefit to be
   A the flexible amount of holiday employees can take.
   B the opportunity to buy or lease a company car.
   C the pension scheme offered by PricewaterhouseCoopers.

7 What impact will *Choices* have on recruitment?
   A It will improve the response to advertised vacancies.
   B It will help the firm recruit the people it wants.
   C It will raise brand awareness among graduates.

8 The main benefit to PricewaterhouseCoopers will be
   A the reduced cost of recruiting new staff.
   B the positive effect on the brand name.
   C the knowledge gained from running the scheme.

PricewaterhouseCoopers, Embankment Place, London

Speaking **3** **Complete the table below with information about *Choices*.**

Advantages for the employee	Advantages for the company
flexible choice	reduces staff turnover

4 **Work in pairs. What benefits could your partner's company introduce? How would they affect the company and its employees?**

choice

performance

A	B	Car
Food	House	324.23
297.62	796.81	311.41
265.81	796.81	354.41
190.93	796.81	

benefit

targets

Staff appraisal

The role of appraisals

Speaking ❶ Do you have appraisals in your company? What is their purpose?

❷ Work in pairs. Look at the list of reasons for appraising staff. Which do you think are the three most important? Why?

- to assess training and development needs
- to help improve current performance
- to review past performance
- to assess promotion prospects
- to set performance objectives
- to review pay

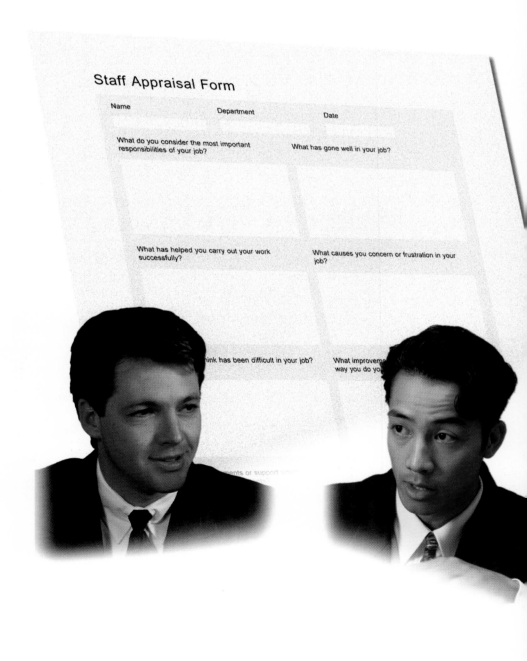

Staff Appraisal Form

Name   Department   Date

What do you consider the most important responsibilities of your job?

What has gone well in your job?

What has helped you carry out your work successfully?

What causes you concern or frustration in your job?

...ink has been difficult in your job?

What improveme... way you do yo...

...ents or suppor...

Listening ❸ Five people talk about their appraisals. Listen and decide the main topic of each extract.

1 .....

2 .....

3 .....

4 .....

5 .....

A	current performance
B	future targets
C	job description
D	past performance
E	pay
F	promotion prospects
G	training
H	working environment

Speaking ❹ How can you ensure the success of an appraisal? What can be done before, during and after the appraisal interview?

Monitoring performance

Reading Read the article about a computerised staff appraisal system. What are the similarities and differences between this system and traditional appraisal methods?

FINANCIAL TIMES   MONDAY OCTOBER 19 1998   ★

INSIDE TRAC

APPRAISAL SYSTEMS

When the system becomes the monitor

Roger Taylor looks at a continuous appraisal system that won't take no for an answer

 Imagine if every time you came back from an appraisal or training course, full of promises to listen to your staff more and be a better manager, somebody actually made sure you carried out your promises. And imagine if that person went around asking colleagues to point out where you had missed your targets. And then sent this information straight to your boss.

This is the dream of Pensare, a small company in Los Altos, California. The company is developing software which uses corporate networks to help managers train and appraise employees - and so enable them to get the most from their human resources budget. What makes the Pensare approach different is the extent to which the program can co-ordinate goals across an organisation and continuously assess those goals.

2 Pensare's course involves a set of online interactive training sessions that take you through the basics - everything from personal development issues to co-ordinating departmental goals with corporate strategy.

The system evaluates your development needs and sets a very wide range of targets, from personal objectives to how your work fits in with the broadest corporate strategy.

3 Now comes the scary part. Not only will the system harass

> **The system will harass you with e-mails and can e-mail your boss if it does not get the answers it wants**

you with e-mails to make sure that you achieve your targets, but it can also be set to e-mail your boss if it does not get the answers it wants. What is more, it is designed to encourage your colleagues to comment on your goals and performance. These comments can be automatically copied to your supervisors along with updates on progress towards meeting targets. In

addition, the system maintains noticeboards where employees can praise or criticise instances of good and bad practice within the company. If all this sounds a little too much like living in a police state, Pensare stresses that the course is fully adaptable to suit any corporate culture.

4 But do not panic. There is still a good chance that even where companies do adopt the Pensare system, employees will not take any notice and the system will fall into disuse. Then we can all happily go back to forgetting appraisals and seminars the moment we leave the room and criticising our workmates in hushed voices while standing around the water cooler.

*Taken from the **Financial Times**, 19 October 199.*

2 Choose the best title for each numbered paragraph.

Paragraph 1 .....

Paragraph 2 .....

Paragraph 3 .....

Paragraph 4 .....

   A   Appraising the boss

   B   Assessing needs and setting aims

   C   Getting the most from your colleagues

   D   Giving feedback

   E   Ignoring the system

   F   Making technology pay

   G   Missing your targets

3 Using the information in the article, complete each sentence with a phrase from the list.

1 At the start of the process, employees have to ...

2 In the next stage, employees are required to ...

3 If employees fail to respond to enquiries about targets, the system will ...

4 The system includes noticeboards where employees can ...

   A   send an e-mail to their boss.

   B   work towards a set of given objectives.

   C   check progress automatically.

   D   do a course of computer-based lessons.

   E   get feedback from their colleagues.

   F   co-ordinate goals within the whole company.

   G   give feedback on what happens in the company.

Speaking **4** Answer the following questions.

1 How effective do you think the Pensare system is?

2 How would you feel if your company implemented a system like Pensare's?

3 What problems could the Pensare system cause?

❶ Read through the unit and the tapescript. Find more benefits.

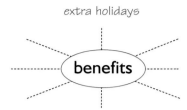

extra holidays

benefits

❷ Match the words.

1	call	power
2	pension	centre
3	lump	costs
4	bargaining	leave
5	payroll	discount
6	annual	scheme
7	bulk	turnover
8	staff	sum

❸ Complete each sentence with the correct form of the word in capital letters.

1 DIVERSE

The system recognises the _____ of all our employees.

2 IMPLEMENT

The _____ of the system took longer than expected.

3 MAINTAIN

Our _____ Department looks after any kind of problem like that.

4 CHALLENGE

After the merger took place, we had to answer a lot of _____ questions from employees.

5 OPTION

The other benefits are all _____ .

6 RECRUIT

We need to focus on _____ .

7 SECURE

The health insurance gives me and my family some financial _____ , which is important.

8 AWARE

The booklet helped raise _____ .

❹ Complete each sentence with a suitable preposition.

1 You can choose according _____ your needs.

2 I've decided to take some time _____ .

3 We hope staff will participate _____ the scheme.

4 One advantage _____ the scheme is its flexibility.

5 The scheme caters _____ all types of employees

6 There's been a lot of interest _____ the scheme.

7 The scheme has had an effect _____ recruitment

8 I took extra holidays in exchange _____ base pay

Gerunds and infinitives

❺ Complete the text with the gerund or infinitive.

The advantages of flexible benefits

Saving you time and money

The concept of flexible benefits is straightforward. They give you the opportunity (**1** *put*) _____ together the mix of pay and benefits that best suits you. As well as (**2** *provide*) _____ you with an easy way of (**3** *meet*) _____ your own individual needs, flexible benefits allow you (**4** *select*) _____ benefits such as a company car, insurance or childcare vouchers, which can save you money. You are very likely (**5** *find*) _____ that the options available are things you have already considered (**6** *purchase*) _____ , such as medical insurance. Our exhaustive research helps you (**7** *make*) _____ the right decisions without (**8** *have*) _____ to do all the work yourself.

Giving you peace of mind

(**9** *Choose*) _____ the right insurance provider can be difficult for anyone not used to (**10** *deal*) _____ with such matters. That is why we are always extremely careful (**11** *select*) _____ only the best providers.

Meeting your changing needs

The real beauty of the flexible benefits system is that it lets you (**12** *review*) _____ your options every twelve months, which means you can change your benefits (**13** *suit*) _____ your changing lifestyle.

Use the words to write sentences with
target/objective.

Unfortunately, we missed last year's sales target.

(un)realistic

meet   miss

last/this/next year's

achieve   set

review   target/   current
                objective

concentrate on   future

co-ordinate

sales   range

work towards

Choose the correct word to complete each sentence.

1 We want a system which will (*ensure/assure*) success.

2 My boss was full of (*praise/criticism*) and said I should consider taking on more responsibility.

3 We managed to (*achieve/meet*) all our deadlines this year.

4 We (*estimated/evaluated*) last year's performance at my appraisal.

5 I complained about my workload, so we had a detailed look at my (*description/duties*).

6 We discussed my (*progress/promotion*) prospects.

7 Could you (*update/remind*) me on our performance so far this year?

8 We don't have a formal training (*culture/policy*).

Complete the appraisal questions with the correct form of the following words. Then answer the questions about yourself.

> frustrate develop success responsible good

1 What are the most important <u>responsibilities</u> in your job?

2 What has gone _____ in your job over the past year?

3 What helps you do your job _____ ?

4 What causes you concern or _____ ?

5 How would you like your job to _____ in the future?

4 You are a manager of an electrical goods wholesaler. Due to a computer error, you have not paid an important supplier's invoice. Write a fax of **30-40 words** to the supplier:

* apologising for the mistake
* explaining how it happened
* saying when the invoice will be paid.

Reporting speech

5 Put the following reporting verbs into the categories below. Use the tapescript to help you.

say	tell	explain	complain
ask	promise	mention	agree

+ (that)	+ infinitive	+object + infinitive	+ about
say		ask someone to ...	

Now use the verbs to report these statements.

1 'Could you arrange a meeting for Friday?'
   <u>She asked me to arrange a meeting for Friday.</u>

2 'Don't worry, I'll send the report today.'
   _____

3 'I'm not happy with the amount of feedback I get.'
   _____

4 'The mistake was due to a computer error.'
   _____

5 'Don't mention pay at the start of the appraisal.'
   _____

6 'OK. You're probably right. We'll raise the price.'
   _____

7 'Could you look for a suitable venue, please?'
   _____

8 'Oh by the way, there's a trade fair on next week.'

Reading Test Part Two

- Read the article below about corporate travel.
- Choose the correct sentence from **A - I** to fill each gap.
- For each gap **1 - 5**, mark **one** letter **A - I**.
- Do not use any letter more than once.

Airlines look to make loyalty pay

The high-flying lifestyle of corporate travel addicts is under threat. Driven from their natural environment of the airport business lounge, they can be seen comparing air mile accounts in ordinary departure lounges across Europe. **(0)** ..... The more air miles an executive had, the more willing he was to put himself out for the good of the company. However, the travel budget has become the latest target of the corporate cost-cutter.

Increasingly, cost-conscious companies are now looking for ways of reducing both the amount and the cost of corporate travel. **(1)** ..... Facilities such as e-mail and video-conferencing, for example, mean that information can be distributed and responded to far more quickly, reducing the need for face-to-face meetings. Cheaper telecommunications will mean that 'virtual meetings', using video-conferencing, will undoubtedly become more common.

Even when journeys are unavoidable, the club-class ticket is no longer guaranteed. More and more executives now find their full-fare business class tickets replaced by discounted promotional tickets or even economy class seats. **(2)** ..... It also affects their ability to collect air miles.

Some airlines have reacted by enlarging their loyalty schemes to include economy flights as well. **(3)** ..... The only problem with doing so is that it often means ignoring company travel policy by booking flights with non-approved airlines.

The attraction of air miles is easy to understand. **(4)** ..... With these benefits in mind, it is easy to see why gold or platinum card holders may be tempted to take extra trips to retain this preferential treatment. When the card is due for renewal, some corporate travellers will always find an excuse for a full-fare business ticket with their favourite carrier.

These executives will be happy to hear that many of the major airlines are looking to form reward scheme alliances. **(5)** ..... For airlines, loyalty schemes such as air miles are no longer a way of filling empty seats, but an important source of revenue.

The schemes also provide airlines with useful information about their customers. Airlines such as British Airways, Lufthansa and KLM all have relationship marketing departments that use this information to build detailed profiles of scheme members. This allows them to approach the right person with the right product at the right time.

Example

0 A B C D E F G H **I**

A   There is a fast growing trade in the sale of unused air miles.

B   For frequent flyers this means more than just reduced levels of comfort.

C   As well as free flights, they provide access to airport lounges and priority on over-booked flights.

D   Business travellers in the United States are often members of four or five reward schemes.

E   With communications systems cheaper and easier to use, many journeys are now unnecessary.

F   United Airlines Mileage Plus members, for example, are recognised by partner airlines such as Lufthansa, Air Canada and SAS.

G   Preventing an executive from earning air miles can even result in resignation.

H   This means air mileage addicts can shop around for the best deal and still add miles to their accounts.

I   Traditionally, frequent flying was seen as a measure of commitment to the company cause.

Writing Test Part Two

- You work in the Sales Department of an international company. Manuela Garcia, an important client, is visiting your company for a day. There are some changes to the itinerary you sent her last week.
- Write a letter of **100 - 120 words** to Ms Garcia, using the original itinerary and your handwritten notes, informing her of the changes.

Proposed itinerary for one-day visit of Manuela Garcia

Wednesday 20 October

11.00	Ms Garcia arrives on flight IB432 from Madrid
	John Sallis to meet Ms Garcia at airport
~~11.30~~ 45	Arrival at company — *Original arrival time too optimistic.*
	John Sallis to give Ms Garcia an introductory tour of company
12.30	Lunch at White Hart restaurant — *Restaurant full. It's now the Swan Hotel.*
	(John Sallis, Carol Snape, Tom McAllister, Sue Smith, Manuela Garcia)
14.00	Meeting in boardroom — *Carol can't make it. Explain why.*
	(Carol Snape, Tom McAllister, Sue Smith, Manuela Garcia)
15.30	Coffee break — *Give some details.*
16.00	Product presentation
	(Carol Snape, Tom McAllister, Sue Smith, Manuela Garcia)
18.00	John Sallis to take Ms Garcia to the airport — *John has to go early. Sue will take Manuela to the airport.*
19.30	Ms Garcia departs on flight IB886 to Madrid

Unit 10a

Marketing disasters

The marketing mix

Speaking ❶ How would the four Ps of marketing - Product, Place, Promotion and Price - apply to the product below?

SOLARIS HOLIDAYS

the

freedom

to be ...

Mauritius
Thailand
Maldives
Seychelles
Virgin Islands
New Zealand
Caribbean
Bahamas
Australia

tel: 0800 96 97 98   www.solaris.com

Reading 1 ❷ Look at the four stories on the opposite page about marketing disasters. Which story does each piece of marketing advice below refer to?

1 Don't change something which is already a proven success.
2 Don't spend more on the promotion than the product.
3 Don't let competitors dictate your strategy.
4 If things go wrong, change the name.
5 A marketing mistake can put a company out of business.
6 Doing things too quickly can produce disastrous results.
7 Work out the exact cost of a promotional gift.

A good idea at the time ...

Some marketing ideas seem heaven sent. But what happens when they become promotions from hell?
***Adrian Stoppard** reports.*

Every advertising executive knows that golden moment when inspiration strikes and the 'perfect' idea appears out of the blue. However, as the following examples show, it is easy to get carried away with the excitement and not think things through carefully enough.

A Cleaned out

Hoover offered any customer who spent at least £100 on its products two complimentary flights to Europe and the US. The offer attracted more than double the anticipated applications, leading to the dismissal of three senior managers and a bill for £19m.

B Another one bytes the dust

A large computer hardware retailer positioned itself at the bottom end of the market by undercutting all its competitors. To attract customers, it even offered a 0% interest Buy Now, Pay One Year Later deal. People did buy, but unfortunately, serious cash flow problems forced the company into liquidation before customers repaid them.

C Washday blues

Lever Brothers rushed Persil Power onto the market to coincide with a rival company's launch of its own new washing powder. Despite millions of pounds spent on research, Persil Power was fatally flawed, having the unfortunate effect of damaging clothes. It was quickly withdrawn and reformulated.

D The unreal thing

'The best has been made even better,' said the Chairman of Coca-Cola about its decision to change the flavour of Coke for the first time in its 99-year history. However, of the 150 million people who tried the new Coke, nearly two-thirds preferred the original. The company was forced to re-launch the old Coke as Coke Classic three months later.

21

Speaking ❸ How could the companies have avoided these mistakes?

Promotions that failed

1 **Work in pairs. Read these stories about promotions that failed. How do you think each story ended?**

Promotion A

A well-known manufacturer of confectionery organised a treasure hunt, which was long considered by the marketing industry as the 'promotion from hell'. The company buried a number of small boxes around the country - their locations to be found in a book of clues. The finder of each box would receive a prize of £10,000.

Promotion B

A petrol station chain wanted to boost sales in a particular town in Scotland where competitors were winning market share. Its Marketing Department came up with what they thought was an imaginative yet safe promotion. The petrol station in question would offer free fuel to any two customers that looked like each other.

Promotion C

A well-known building company ran a competition as part of its campaign to attract customers. The winner of the first prize would receive a top-of-the-range conservatory plus garden furniture and a barbecue set. Thousands of people entered the competition.

2 **Now ask your teacher YES/NO questions to discover what went wrong.**

Marketing disasters

Listening **3** Three people talk about the failed promotions. Listen and decide which promotion each person is talking about.

1 .....

2 .....

3 .....

Grammar **4** Look at the tapescript and underline all the examples of conditional forms.

Don't forget!

Expressing hindsight

We can talk about past mistakes in the following ways.

With hindsight, we should have/could have ...

What we should have/could have done is ...

If we'd ..., we wouldn't have ...

Speaking **5** Work in pairs. Look at the promotions again. Which disaster would have been the easiest/most difficult to avoid? Explain why.

6 Think of other stories about marketing disasters or failed products. Which of the four Ps of marketing did the companies get wrong? What should they have done?

Unit 10b

Going global

Choosing the right product

Speaking ❶ Think of three successful products. Why are they successful?

❷ Put each of the three products in the appropriate quarter of the framework below. Which products are most suitable for globalisation?

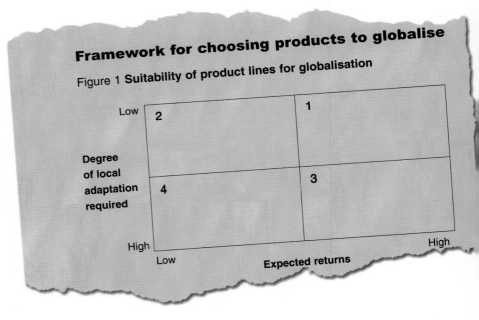

❸ In the 1980s the US hotel group Marriott Corporation decided on a strategy of globalisation. Put these Marriott brands into the framework.

- 'Marriott' brand (full-service hotels)
- 'Courtyard' brand (mid-price hotels)
- 'Residence Inn' brand (long-term-stay hotels)
- Marriott Senior Living Services (retirement communities)

10 Mastering **Global Business**

Case study

Marriott

As the company began its globalisation, it had to decide which product lines to start with. Figure 1 represents a framework to identify those product lines suitable for early globalisation. As indicated, each line of business in the company's portfolio should be evaluated along two dimensions - potential pay-off (expected returns) and potential risk (degree of local adaptation required).

The first dimension focuses on the potential profits of globalisation. In Marriott's case, the two products with the highest margins are its full-service hotels (the 'Marriott' brand) and long-term-stay hotels (the 'Residence Inn' brand). In a business such as the Marriott hotels, where the principal customers are globetrotting corporate executives, a worldwide presence can create significant value because the company can use a centralised reservations system and develop globally standardised services which assure customers of high quality.

The second dimension refers to the level of adaptation required to enter foreign markets. Since any new development involves risk, the greater the degree of local adaptation required, the greater the risk of failure. For the Marriott Corporation, both its 'Marriott' and 'Courtyard' brands could successfully offer globally standardised services, whereas the retirement communities and the long-term-stay hotels would require far more local adaptation.

Thus, full-service hotels offer both a greater pay-off and less risk and are therefore the best candidate for globalisation.

Framework for c

Adapted from the Financial Times, 30 January 1998

Speaking ⑤ Work in pairs. Discuss the following questions.

1 How can a worldwide presence add value to a company?
2 What are the risks involved in adapting a product for a foreign market?

Entering the market

Listening ❶ Donald Fraser, a consultant at Kennedy, McLeish & Partners (KMP), talks about advising companies on exporting. Listen and choose one letter for the correct answer.

1 Companies approach KMP for advice on choosing
  A the right products to export.
  B the most suitable foreign market.
  C the best way of entering a market.

2 The safest method for a company to enter a foreign market is
  A having an agreement with a local company.
  B setting up its own local production.
  C finding a joint venture partner.

3   What is the main advantage of joint ventures?
   A   They are the cheapest way of entering a market.
   B   They are a risk-free way of doing business.
   C   They provide important market knowledge.

4   The danger with a joint venture is that one company might
   A   refuse to share know-how with the other partner.
   B   use the arrangement as the basis for a takeover.
   C   exploit and then leave the other partner.

5   A subsidiary is the best way of entering a market when
   A   high sales volumes are expected.
   B   the products are cheap to produce.
   C   a foreign market is near home.

6   Companies can improve their chances of success by
   A   developing new products exclusively for the market.
   B   changing the product to suit the target market.
   C   using designers recruited from the target market.

Donald Fra
Kennedy, McLeish & Partn

7   A company is forced to expand quickly when
   A   cheaper competition appears on the market.
   B   it has a successful formula that sells well.
   C   its production costs are very high.

8   Donald advises companies to prepare for expansion by
   A   training their key managers.
   B   having a comprehensive business plan.
   C   assessing their financial resources.

2 **What are the advantages and disadvantages of the following ways of entering a market?**

Franchise	Joint venture	Wholly-owned subsidiary
lower financial risk	can share costs and risks	complete control

Speaking **3** **Work in pairs. Find out whether your partner's company exports its products/services. Why did the company choose those particular products/services? How did it enter the foreign markets?**

Going global

Speaking **4** Play the game in groups. Your company decides to globalise its operations. Choose a counter to represent your export product. Then choose a market. Add up your total income as you move around the board. When you land on a Report square, another student will read a card to you. The game is over when one player reaches FINISH. The winner is the person with the most money.

globalise
SYDNEY

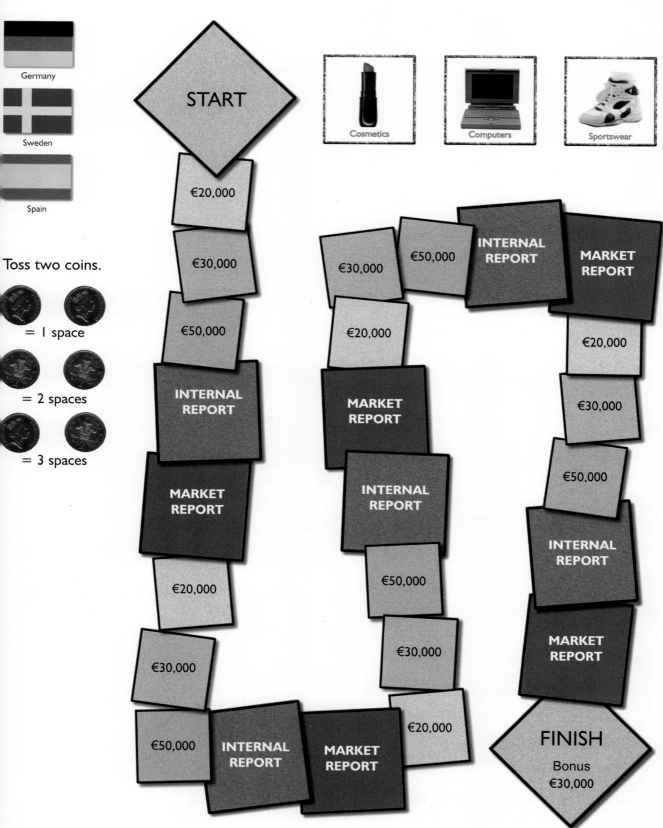

Germany

Sweden

Spain

Toss two coins.

= 1 space

= 2 spaces

= 3 spaces

START

Cosmetics

Computers

Sportswear

€20,000

€30,000

€50,000

INTERNAL REPORT

MARKET REPORT

€20,000

€30,000

€50,000

€30,000

€50,000

INTERNAL REPORT

MARKET REPORT

€20,000

€30,000

€50,000

MARKET REPORT

INTERNAL REPORT

€50,000

€30,000

INTERNAL REPORT

MARKET REPORT

€50,000

INTERNAL REPORT

MARKET REPORT

€20,000

FINISH

Bonus €30,000

1 Read through the unit and the tapescript. Find more words and phrases connected with *promotion*.

to attract
customers / interest   to offer a prize

promotion

2 Complete the sentences with *market* or *marketing*.

1 The company positioned itself at the bottom end of the _____ .

2 A _____ failure can put a company out of business.

3 He's the manager of the _____ Department.

4 A rival company stole their _____ share.

5 They rushed their new product onto the _____ before they had fully tested it.

3 Match the words.

1 boost ───────────── a product
2 undercut ───────── sales
3 attract   competitors
4 withdraw   market share
5 run   customers
6 avoid   a competition
7 win   mistakes

Now complete the sentences with the combinations.

1 They plan to _____ where the top prize is a flight to the USA.

2 They're hoping the promotion will _____ away from competitors.

3 A good promotion can _____ by as much as 3 or 4 per cent.

4 We have 10 per cent of the market and plan to _____ by focusing on price.

5 They planned to lower prices and _____ in order to win customers.

6 Sometimes you can't _____ because you can't anticipate everything that could go wrong.

7 They had to _____ two days before the launch because it was fatally flawed.

Conditional 3

4 Look at the three stories on page 133 about promotions that failed. Then complete the sentences.

The confectionery company

1 could have   *considered the promotion* *more carefully.*

2 should have   _____
_____

The petrol station chain

3 shouldn't have _____
_____

4 could have   _____
_____

The building company

5 should have   _____
_____

6 shouldn't have _____
_____

5 Write complete sentences from the prompts.

1 Hoover's offer / not such a disaster / if / not offer / such a good prize

   Hoover's offer wouldn't have been such a *disaster if they hadn't offered such a good prize.*

2 senior managers / keep their jobs / if / company / not lose / so much money

   _____
   _____

3 if / customers / repay / computer retailer / earlier / it / not go / out of business

   _____
   _____

4 if / customers / not prefer / original flavour / Coke / not have to / relaunch / it

   _____
   _____

Match the words to make compound nouns.

1 pay- ———————— over
2 know- ———————→ off
3 joint   building
4 take   venture
5 decision-   how
6 team-   making

Match the words to make compound adjectives. Then think of a noun to go after each adjective.

1 mid- ———————— wide
2 long- ———————→ price   *hotel*
3 world   free
4 wholly-   margin
5 risk-   term
6 high   owned

Use the words to write sentences with *market*.

We need advice on entering our target market.

Russian

global   export

enter   target

consumer   (market)   knowledge

local   share

grow   report

presence

Rewrite each of the sentences without changing its meaning. Use a form of the word in italics.

1 They decided on a *global* approach to operations.
   They decided to ____globalise____ operations.

2 We *acquired* a company last year.
   We _____ last year.

3 They *failed* to adapt.
   There was _____ to adapt.

4 They *own* the company completely.
   They have _____ the company.

5 We agreed to *license* our products.
   We signed a _____ .

Grammar review

5 Complete the memo. Put the words in brackets into a suitable form.

To: Amy Majors
From: Joe Petrescu

Thanks for the information about the Brazilian market, which you (1 *send*) ____sent____ last week. I (2 *only/manage*) _____ to have a quick look at it so far, but it (3 *look*) _____ interesting. I (4 *speak*) _____ to Dale yesterday and he (5 *think*) _____ we should organise a meeting to discuss our strategy for (6 *enter*) _____ the Brazilian market. He (7 *travel*) _____ to Mexico next week, but he's free on 10 May. Could you attend a meeting then? It seems that our joint venture in Mexico (8 *do*) _____ very well in the last few months and we (9 *learn*) _____ a lot from it. In fact, Dale is so confident about the way things (10 *go*) _____ in Latin America that he would like us (11 *enter*) _____ Brazil on a 60-40 basis. The feeling is that if we have a controlling interest this time, we (12 *avoid*) _____ one or two of the problems we (13 *experience*) _____ when we first set up operations in Mexico.

6 Correct the mistake in each sentence below.

1   I need some informations about the meeting.
2   Their news were very encouraging.
3   It's the service what really matters.
4   I look forward to hear from you in due course.
5   This type of problem is very normally.
6   We are very interesting in your product range.
7   I didn't manage finishing all the work on time.
8   Who's offer did you finally decide to accept?
9   The report bases on the most recent figures.
10 The company is a lot bigger as it used to be.
11 Last year's sales figures have to be checking.
12 So the company's doing well, does it?
13 It's a lot more harder to find clients than keep them.
14 She didn't give me many advice on what to do.
15 When I told him the problem, he said me that it wasn't important.

Listening Test Part One

Questions 1 - 12

- You will hear three telephone conversations.
- Write **one or two** words or a number in the numbered spaces on the forms below.
- You will hear each conversation twice.

Conversation One
(Questions 1 - 4)

- Look at the form below.
- You will hear a woman placing an order for office supplies.

Customer Order Form	*Order Reference*	*XR 4930*
	Date Received	*27/5/99*

Customer Name — *Lacey Graphics*

Delivery Address — **(1)** ....

Hailsham Industrial Estate

Hailsham

For the attention of: **(2)** ....

Order Details — *10 boxes of* **(3)** ....

Delivery Date — **(4)** ....

Payment Method — *Invoice*

Conversation Two
(Questions 5 - 8)

- Look at the form below.
- You will hear a woman checking details about a job advertisement.

Computer hardware wholesaler requires a **(5)** .... for immediate

employment. **(6)** .... + benefits.

Applicants should include full CV, references and details of **(7)** ....

Interviews to be held in the week commencing **(8)** ....

Closing date for applications 17 March.

Conversation Three
(Questions 9 - 12)

- Look at the form below.
- You will hear a man checking details of his appointments.

FRENCH BUSINESS TRIP: Wed 2/10 - Fri 4/10

Appointments

11.30   Meeting at Maplo with **(9)** ....

         She's their new **(10)** ....

15.30   Meet Monsieur Belois at **(11)** .... to discuss new products.

Don't forget

Call office tomorrow.

(12) .... to Rome on Friday.

Listening Test Part Two

Questions 13 - 22

Section One
(Questions 13 - 17)

- You will hear five telephone calls.
- For each piece, decide which place **A - H** each speaker is at.
- Write **one** letter **A - H** next to the number of the piece.
- Do not use any letter more than once.
- You will hear the five pieces twice.

13   .....

14   .....

15   .....

16   .....

17   .....

A	bank
B	car hire company
C	credit card company
D	insurance company
E	office letting agency
F	office stationer's
G	parcel carrier office
H	travel agency

Section Two
(Questions 18 - 22)

- You will hear another five short pieces.
- For each piece, decide what the speaker is trying to do **A - H**.
- Write **one** letter **A - H** next to the number of the piece.
- Do not use any letter more than once.
- You will hear the five pieces twice.

18 .....

19 .....

20 .....

21 .....

22 .....

A	make an enquiry
B	offer help
C	cancel an appointment
D	accept an invitation
E	refuse an offer
F	confirm information
G	make a complaint
H	change an order

Listening Test Part Three

Questions 23 - 30

- You will hear a radio interview about health and safety fines in the workplace.
- For each question, **23 - 30**, choose one letter **A**, **B** or **C** for the correct answer.
- You will hear the interview twice.

23 In general, current health and safety standards are now

    A worse than before.

    B the same as before.

    C better than before.

24 Mr Hayes believes that current fines are

    A too high.

    B fair.

    C too low.

25 Unlimited fines can only be imposed by the

    A Crown Court.

    B Health and Safety Commission.

    C Magistrates Courts.

26 The main purpose of higher fines would be to

    A put the worst offenders out of business.

    B punish companies that have offended.

    C stop other companies from offending.

27 Mr Hayes believes that fines should be set according to

   A the size of the company.

   B the seriousness of the offence.

   C the ability of the company to pay.

28 How many cases did local authorities win against companies?

   A They have won only a few.

   B They have won almost all.

   C They have won all.

29 The average penalty companies had to pay was about

   A £1,000.

   B £1,500.

   C £2,000.

30 In the last few years, the number of cases against companies has

   A decreased steadily.

   B remained unchanged.

   C increased slightly.

Reading Test Part Five Section B

- Read the job advertisement below.
- In **each** line there is **one wrong word**.
- For each numbered line **1 - 5**, write the **correct word in CAPITAL LETTERS**.

Example

0	A						

00	O	F					

0 The successful applicant will be the graduate with suitable, recognised

00 European qualifications and a minimum five years' experience at

1 investment products. Individuals are too likely to have a good working

2 knowledge of marketing. Each candidates are expected to show good

3 communication skills, and a basic knowledge of at less three European

4 languages would be an advantage. Furthermore, the ability for work in a

5 multicultural team is of key importance. That successful candidate

   may be based in either London or Frankfurt.

Your company is looking for new offices. Exchange information with your partner about two possible office sites.

Your questions

Ask your partner for this information about an office in Berlin.

Cost	....
Availability	....
Amenities	....

Your information

Your partner will ask you questions about this office in Milan. Use the information below to answer the questions.

OFFICE TO LET: MILAN

Size: 200 sq.m.

Ground floor

Situated on busy shopping street

Recently renovated and in excellent condition

Excellent amenities including air conditioning
and underground car parking

Viewing by appointment only through agents

You are Gina Theismann. You have just received Tom's fax about the meeting in London. The dates are not very convenient for your team members, Steve Cerny and Joni Morgan. Telephone Tom and arrange a new date for the meeting in London. Use the availability table below.

February	2 3 4 5 6	9 10 11 12 13	16 17 18 19 20	23 24 25 26 27
Steve	Holiday			Rome
Joni	IL2 project			

❶ You need to speak to your company's Head of Central European Sales, Hanna Kwasniewski. Telephone her to:

- confirm the venue and dates of the European Sales Conference
- ask her to send the regional sales figures
- say when you need the figures.

❷ You work for Socotel in Paris. There is a call for your colleague, Colette Contart, who is ill today. Take a message.

WHILE YOU WERE OUT

To: .... Date: ....

From: .... Company: ....

Tel: ....

Returned your call ☐   Please ring back ☐   Will ring back ☐

MESSAGE

....
....
....
....
....

Complete the graph that your partner describes.

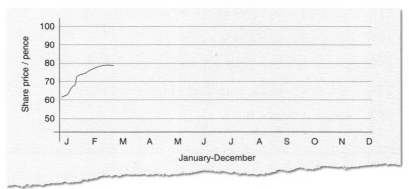

Describe the bar chart below to your partner.

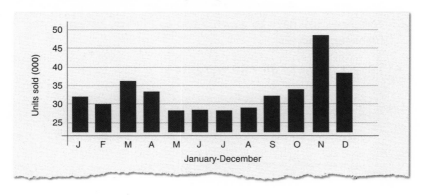

Unit 6b

Environmental questionnaire assessment

0-8   The company probably does not even realise that it has an impact on the environment. Management obviously has no idea about or interest in environmental performance.

8-16   Although the company thinks about environmental matters, it has no formal policy or clear understanding of how to reduce its environmental impact. But at least the company recognises the fact that it has an impact.

16-24   The company is taking the simple but necessary action required to protect and preserve our natural world. In future, these actions will be standard practice for all companies.

Unit 7a

Injuries in the office

The figures below from a 1997 UK Health and Safety Executive report show a breakdown of the most common injuries in the office.

Office Injuries 1991-1997

In the UK, in the six-year period to 1997, there were 3,657 injuries to employees which resulted in them being absent from work for more than 3 days.

Table 1: Causes of over 3-day injuries in the office

12%   resulted from being struck by a moving object.

15%   resulted from a fall from a height.

35%   resulted from handling, lifting or carrying an object.

7%   resulted from the person striking a fixed object.

25%   resulted from a slip or trip.

Writing Test

- You are the Assistant Sales Manager of a large engineering company. You have to go on a trip to Munich instead of the Sales Manager, who is ill.

- Write a memo of **30 - 40** words to your sales team:

  *   explaining why you will be away
  *   telling them when you will be back
  *   suggesting an alternative day and time for the next sales meeting.

Candidate A

Your Questions

You need to ask Candidate B for this information about a company that you are interested in buying.

Activities	....
Location	....
Company weaknesses	....

Information

This is the information about another company. Try to answer candidate B's questions.

Company Profile

Kleinfeld & Marsh

Auditors and management consultants

Offices in Amsterdam (HQ), Brussels and London

Total of 210 employees in all three offices

Turnover last year €24m

All three offices occupied on long-term leases

Good client list, including several blue chip European companies

Strengths:	*Young motivated staff*
	Large enough to work with international companies
	Excellent track record
Weaknesses:	*Young company, not established name*

Currently valued at €16m

Discussion

Discussion:

Discuss with your partner what is important when considering buying an overseas subsidiary. Think about **price**, **location**, **potential growth** and any other points you think are important.

Candidate A

Your Questions

You need to ask Candidate B for this information about a supplier.

Age	....
Activities	....
Delivery times	....

Information

This is the information about another supplier. Try to answer Candidate B's questions.

Supplier report

Name:	**Palestro Industrial SRL**
Based:	Buenos Aires, Argentina
Established:	Family business founded 50 years ago
Activities:	Manufacturer of components for air conditioning units
Clients:	Mostly in Latin America, some in the USA
Workforce:	Total of 180 employees
Products:	Range of 2,000 components for air conditioning units
Quality:	Good, despite old factory and some old machinery
Prices:	Very reasonable
Delivery:	Could be long on large orders
Contact:	Pedro Palestro

Discussion

Discussion:

Discuss with your partner what is important when considering a supplier. Consider **price**, **reliability**, **location** and any other points you think are important.

Candidate B

Your Questions

You need to ask Candidate A for this information about a supplier.

Location	....
Size	....
Facilities	....

Information

This is the information about another supplier. Try to answer Candidate A's questions.

Supplier report

Name:	**Emicol Eletrõnicos SA**
Based:	São Paulo, Brazil
Established:	1978
Produces:	Specialises in microchips and integrated circuits
Clients:	Has exported to USA and Europe for over 10 years
Size:	One of largest in Latin America
Products:	Total of 15,000 different products
Quality:	Generally very high
Factory:	Up-to-date factory with modern machinery
Delivery:	Can ship many products within two weeks
Prices:	Quite expensive for region, but still competitive

Discussion

Discussion:

Discuss with your partner what is important when considering a supplier. Consider **price**, **reliability**, **location** and any other points you think are important.

Candidate B

Your Questions

You need to ask Candidate A for this information about a company that you are interested in buying.

Number of employees	....
Annual turnover	....
Company strengths	....

Information

This is the information about another company. Try to answer Candidate A's questions.

Company Profile

Koemann Investments

Financial services: pensions, life assurance and personal investments

Turnover last year: €15m

Located in Amsterdam

Total of 38 employees in two offices

Both offices owned on freehold basis

Strengths:	*Has achieved steady growth over last 5 years*
	Over 25 years' experience in investment business
	Asking price is good value
Weaknesses:	*Small company*
	Limited potential for growth

Currently valued at €14m

Discussion

Discussion:

Discuss with your partner what is important when considering buying an overseas subsidiary. Think about **price**, **location**, **potential growth** and any other points you think are important.

Your company is looking for new offices. Exchange information with your partner about two possible office sites.

Your information

Your partner will ask you questions about this office in Berlin. Use the information below to answer the questions.

OFFICE TO LET: BERLIN

Size: 350 sq.m.

Ninth floor office

Cost: DM 40,000 per sq.m. per month

Located in central business area

Renovation and redecoration to be completed by end of September

Amenities: air conditioning and passenger lifts

Your questions

Ask your partner for this information about an office in Milan.

Size	....
Location	....
Condition	....

You are Tom Granger. Gina Theismann phones you about the dates for the meeting in London. Use the availability table below for the Polish team members to finalise a date for the meeting.

February	2 3 4 5 6	9 10 11 12 13	16 17 18 19 20	23 24 25 26 27
Hannah	e-project			
Barbara	Head Office			
Sergiusz			Poznan	

Student B
Unit 1b

1 You work in the Sales Department of your company's Warsaw office. There is a call for Hanna Kwasniewski, the Head of Central European Sales. Hanna is away on business today. Take a message.

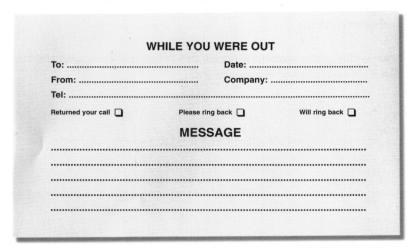

WHILE YOU WERE OUT

To: ....   Date: ....

From: ....   Company: ....

Tel: ....

Returned your call ☐   Please ring back ☐   Will ring back ☐

MESSAGE

....

....

....

....

....

2 You have an appointment with Colette Contart of Socotel on 8 July at 14.00 in Paris. Telephone her to:

- say you are unable to keep the appointment
- apologise and explain why you have to postpone the meeting
- suggest a new date.

Student B
Unit 6a

Describe the graph below to your partner.

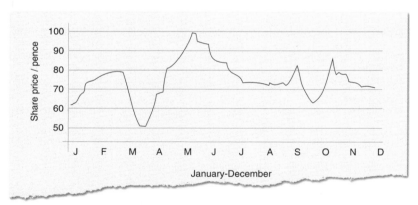

Complete the bar chart that your partner describes.

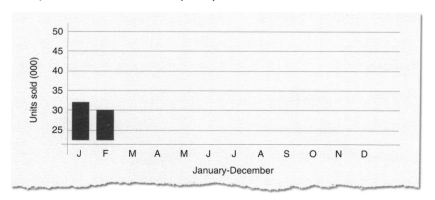

Tapescripts

Unit 1b: Communication

Listening 1

Call 1
Hello Frida. This is Margaret Brock here. It's 9.30 on Wednesday morning. I'm ringing about the half-year sales report. Could you send me a copy of your department's figures, please? I'm in Helsinki until Friday. Thanks very much. Bye.

Call 2
This is Frank Larsen from Scandinavian Conferences in Copenhagen. I'm ringing to tell you that this year's Danish Telecommunications Trade Fair's taking place in the week of November 22. If you'd like some complimentary tickets, please let me know how many you'll need. Please call me on 0045 33 346 766. Thank you. Bye.

Call 3
Hi Frida. It's Sue Mellor. How are you? I hope you're not too busy at the moment. I wanted to talk to you about my visit next month. You know we'd talked about the 13th? Well, I'm afraid it's not going to work out because of deadlines here. I don't suppose we could put it back a week or so, could we? Give me a ring and let me know. Thanks.

Call 4
Hi Frida. It's Colin. I'm on my mobile because I'm travelling to a meeting with a client but I need to talk to you urgently so could you call me on 0486 772 444? It's my mobile number. I need to talk to you about that contract we're trying to get in Helsinki because the customer accepted our proposal and I need to know whether it's all right if I just go ahead and sign the contracts or whether you want to get involved, as well. Could you get back to me asap? Thanks.

Call 5
Hello Frida. It's Steve Montgomery here. I got your proposal for the product launch and I've finally managed to get a look at it. It looks OK, but I think there could still be one or two minor problems with it. I think the time schedule looks a bit on the optimistic side, as well. I've got a couple of suggestions, which I'll get off to you today. Let me know what you think, OK? Bye.

Listening 2

Conversation 1

T = Tom   F = Frida

T   Good afternoon. Scandinavian Conferences.
F   Good afternoon. Could I speak to Frank Larsen, please?
T   I'm afraid he's not here today. Can I help you?
F   I'm ringing about the Danish Telecommunications Trade Fair. Mr Larsen phoned to offer me some tickets and he asked me to let him know how many I'd need.
T   Well, I can send you the tickets. That's no problem. I'll just need your name and address.
F   Right. It's Frida Andersson from Sanderlin. The address is Torshamnsgatan, S-126 25 Stockholm.
T   So, that's Frida Andersson at Torhamnsgatan, S-126 25. OK. How many tickets do you need?
F   Three, please.
T   And which days would you like them for?
F   Just for Tuesday 23 November, please.
T   And could I have the other names for the tickets?
F   I'm afraid I can only confirm two names at the moment. Kati Gersel and myself.
T   Could you spell Gersel, please?
F   Yes, that's G-E-R-S-E-L.
T   Right. I'll put the tickets in the post today.
F   Thanks very much. Bye.
T   Thank you for calling. Goodbye.

Conversation 2

R = Receptionist   F = Frida

R   Good afternoon. Can I help you?
F   Good afternoon. Could I speak to Sue Mellor, please?
R   May I ask who's calling?
F   It's Frida Andersson from Head Office.
R   One moment, please. I'll put you through.
R   Hello?
F   Hello?
R   I'm afraid she's not in her office at the moment. Can I take a message?
F   Yes. Could you tell her that I got her message and I've cancelled our meeting on the 13th. But I'm not available the following week, so I suggest meeting on 27 November.
R   OK. So, that's Frida Andersson from Head Office. The meeting on the 13th is cancelled and you suggest meeting on 27 November instead.
F   That's right. And could she call me to confirm the date?
R   OK. I'll give her the message and she'll get back to you as soon as possible.
F   Thank you.
R   Oh, does she have your number?
F   Yes, she does.
R   OK. Thanks for calling.
F   Thanks. Bye.

Unit 2a: Entertaining a client

Listening 1

1   Fine, thanks. I'm glad you managed to find me somewhere so near the office. That makes things so much easier in the morning. But I have to say, the bed was so hard I didn't get to sleep till two this morning.

2   Pretty awful, actually. There was one delay after another and then I got stopped at Customs. And apparently, my luggage is somewhere between here and Cape Town.

3   Wonderful. I'm really enjoying it here and the people are so friendly. I'll definitely come back for a holiday. But I'll need a week at least next time. Actually, I wouldn't mind living here for a while.

4   Well, I thought it was pretty good from our point of view, but I can see that some people might not be so happy. Still, we got through quite a lot and made some progress. But I still think we're a long way from a decision.

5   OK, but it was a bit too heavy for me. Actually, given a choice, I'd have preferred a salad.

Listening 2

S1 = Speaker 1   S2 = Speaker 2

S1   So, what did you think of the food?
S2   OK, but it was a bit too heavy for me. Actually, given a choice, I'd have preferred a salad.
S1   Salad?
S2   Oh, yes. I don't really eat meat.
S1   What do you have at home? You're not a vegetarian, are you?
S2   Well, I'm not. But my wife is.
S1   Oh, really?
S2   Oh, yes. I haven't had meat at home for years.
S1   Don't you miss it?
S2   Sometimes. But then I go and have a secret steak.

Unit 3a: Ordering goods

Listening

A = Antonella   K = Korinna

A   Pronto, Zanetti.
K   Hello, Antonella?
A   Yes?
K   Hello? It's Korinna Krämer from Otto in Hamburg.
A   Oh, hi Korinna. How are you?
K   Fine, thanks. I'm ringing about the skirts for the summer catalogue.
A   Oh yes. The Cristi and Faci skirts. Did you speak to Mr Hubner?
K   Yes, I did. We definitely want only the standard length.
A   OK. So that's Cristi and Faci in standard length only. Right.
K   And have you spoken to the vendors about quantity yet?
A   No, not yet. I thought I'd wait until we knew what was happening about the lengths.
K   Do you think you could speak to them soon, though? We don't have much time left before the deadline.
A   No problem. I'll call them this morning. And is it still only 400 pieces of each?
K   Yes, that's right.
A   OK. I'll fax you as soon as I've spoken to them.
K   That's great, Antonella. Thanks for your help.
A   That's OK. I'll speak to you later.
K   Great. I'll expect your call then. Bye.

Unit 3b: Cash flow

Listening

B = Barbara   St = Steve   Su = Sue

B   So, Steve, how's the cash flow situation? Any better?
St Not really, no. The more we sell, the less cash we seem to have.
B   Yes, I know. It's called over-trading. You're going to have to figure out a quicker way of turning those sales into cash.
Su But how, Barbara? That's the question.
B   Well, did you think any more about offering early settlement discounts?
St Oh yeah, we talked to most of our customers about it. They sounded quite interested. It seems that if we offered a 1% discount, about half our customers would pay in ten days.
B   Well, that would make a big difference to cash flow.
Su But if we offer 2%, three quarters of our customers will pay within ten days.
B   That's great. So why don't you do it?
St Oh come on, Barbara. Our margins are small enough already. I don't see how we can afford to offer discounts. If we gave a 2% discount, we'd lose thousands of dollars every year.
B   Do you know how much exactly?
St Well, on average monthly sales of $25,000, it'd cost us over four and a half thousand a year.
B   What if you offered 1% and half your customers used it?
St Well, that'd cost us about 1,500 a year. That's a lot of money, Barbara.
B   But don't forget your financing costs, Steve. Financing your cash flow gap means you're paying the bank almost $3,000 a year in interest. I worked out that if you offered the 1% discount, you'd save almost a thousand on financing costs.
Su So what you're saying is the real cost of the discount would only be $500 more?
B   That's right. And your cash flow for the month would increase by over $8,000. And with the 2% discount, you'd have an extra 16,000 a month.

Su Wow. That much? We could really use that extra cash, Steve.
St Hmm. I still think 2% is too much.
Su Then why don't we offer 1%?
St Mmm ... Barbara?
B   Well, it's not my decision. But if I were you Steve, I'd really think very seriously about offering an early settlement discount.
St OK. OK. I get the point. If it really can make that big a difference, we'll give it a try.

Unit 4a: Brand power

Listening 1

1   The thing is, when you buy a car, you're spending a lot of money so you want to get excited about what you're buying. Reliability and after-sales service are all very important, but they're not exactly exciting, are they? I want my car to say something about me. I want something which looks sporty and attracts attention. I don't mind paying that bit extra for something that makes me look good.

2   A lot of my friends have got e-mail so I wanted to buy a computer. I just didn't know much about them, and I found that all that information you get about performance and so on is totally confusing. And then I saw that advert on TV with those new computers. It showed how easy it is to get onto the Internet and send e-mail. So I went to a computer superstore, had a look at one and bought it straightaway.

3   I thought buying a mobile phone would be easy, but it wasn't. You ask how much they cost and you get all this stuff about monthly service contracts and different tariffs at different times of day. It's almost impossible to work out how much they actually cost! Anyway, I worked out that the best deal for me was a one-year all-inclusive package. So that's what I bought.

4   I used to think that one refrigerator was pretty much like any other. But then I saw this TV programme about how much energy kitchen appliances use. Fridges are the worst, apparently. That's because they're on all the time so they're really bad for the ozone layer - all those CFC gases or whatever they call them. So, I decided to get a fridge that doesn't give off lots of harmful gases. And it's cheaper to run as well.

5   It's not even a particularly well-known make of video recorder but I had one of them before which I was really happy with. I didn't have much money when I bought the first one so I just got the cheapest one I could find. But it was great. It lasted years and I never had any problems with it. So, of course, I decided to buy the same brand again. I mean, a friend of mine recently bought a really well-known make and it's been back to the shop twice already.

Listening 2 and 3

// = pause in cassette in Listening 3

I = Interviewer   D = David Noble

I   Now you've set up Sainsbury's Bank, how do you market its products?
D   Well, the core target for Sainsbury's Bank is, quite understandably, the Sainsbury's customer. So, the vast majority of marketing is either in-store or through // direct mail. We've bought very little advertising space, but we do also use // public relations as a marketing tool.
I   And how successful has it been?
D   It's actually exceeded all our expectations. We've already attracted // over 700,000 customers within 12 months of starting trading.
I   Really? And how does a new bank like Sainsbury's succeed in attracting people away from the High Street banks?
D   Quite simply by offering // value for money and excellent customer service standards. I think Reward Points are another big attraction.

With a Sainsbury's Bank Visa Card, for example, a customer can soon collect a lot of Reward Points, which of course can be exchanged for air miles or other kinds of vouchers.

And what makes you think you'll succeed in such a competitive sector?

Well, our key operational advantage is that, as a telephone-only operation, Sainsbury's Bank doesn't have the // high overheads that a branch network does. Therefore, we're able to offer better rates. I think another important point is that Sainsbury's experience in retailing means that its bank can apply a retailer's customer-focused mentality to the financial services sector.

Now some observers say that supermarket chains risk damaging their brands by moving into a sector which they have no experience of. How do you react to that?

Well, that assumes that supermarkets will offer the same poor customer service as the traditional banks and therefore attract the same // bad publicity. As I said, customer service is precisely our strength. We firmly believe that our commitment to our customers will prevent // brand damage.

Yes, other supermarkets obviously feel the same way and we regularly see reports about how they're planning to sell computers, cars and even houses. How do you see the Sainsbury's brand developing in the future?

Well, the brand is continuously evolving and developing. The move into financial services is another stage of that ongoing development. When you look back at the history of the // Sainsbury's brand, it's already been developed in many different ways. Who could have imagined, back in 1869, that a small family dairy would grow into a // major retail group operating over 800 stores? I've no doubt that the brand will continue to develop, but it's difficult to say exactly how.

Unit 4b: Public relations

Listening 1

J = Journalist   E = Eilish O'Shea

J   So Eilish, maybe you could begin by telling us about your duties as the PR Manager.

E   Well, my job is to plan and manage the public relations strategy for the Skoda brand in the UK. This means I'm responsible for dealing with the press, television and radio, as well as communications with the public and personnel in our UK dealerships.

J   How would you describe the role of the PR Department within the company?

E   Well, the primary role of PR is to create understanding with the public. My job involves talking and listening to both the press and the public, providing them with information from the heart of the organisation. Our objective is to give an accurate picture of the company, its brands and what it believes in. We have to make sure that the public has a positive image of the company.

J   So how does this role differ from that of the Marketing Department?

E   Marketing has more to do with identifying customer needs and developing the right products to satisfy those needs. PR, on the other hand, is more concerned with establishing and maintaining goodwill and understanding between the company and its public. Marketing reaches the public through advertising, whereas we work more with the press and broadcast media.

J   But how much control do you have over what the press says?

E   None really. But that's what makes the way we deal with the press so important. Our job is to make sure that journalists always have a very clear understanding of what the company is trying to do. Maintaining good relationships with the press is a very important part of the job. In PR you have to build long-term relationships with journalists because you work with them on a regular basis and trust is absolutely essential.

Listening 2

J = Journalist   E = Eilish O'Shea

J   When Skoda relaunched its brand here in 1995, it would be fair to say that the company had a genuine image problem. How big a challenge was this for the PR Department?

E   Unfortunately, Skoda was misunderstood by the UK public at the time. There used to be a lot of boring old jokes about Skoda cars. But that was because of people's misconceptions about the quality of central European engineering. The strange thing is that the reality was actually quite different.

J   In what way?

E   Well, central Europe had always been a centre of engineering excellence. However, from the start of the communist era in 1948 it had to develop on its own without the benefit of outside influence and up-to-date technology.

J   So how did you go about communicating this reality to the public?

E   When we re-entered the UK marketplace with a new model, the Felicia, in 1995, we put a huge emphasis on advertising, everything from national advertising to point-of-sale material in the showrooms. This was repeated with the arrival of the Octavia in 1998. Our overall aim was to communicate the quality of Skoda.

J   And what role did the PR Department play?

E   Well, regardless of how successful and effective advertising is, the public is always aware that the company has complete control over the message and content of the advert. However, when the public reads positive things in their favourite magazine or newspaper, it's the journalist's own comment and therefore much more powerful because it isn't influenced by the organisation. So, our job was to communicate the quality of Skoda to the motoring press.

J   Having seen the very positive press the company now enjoys, you obviously managed to do that. But how?

E   One of the first press events we arranged was a trip to see the manufacturing plant in the Czech Republic. We took almost 100 journalists with us to show them just how good the facility was. We organised a similar trip the following year to see the new Octavia plant, which is one of the most modern in the world. These trips really changed people's attitudes.

J   Well, you certainly won over the press. But what kind of feedback have you had from the public?

E   Well, Skoda recently came top of a major consumer magazine's annual survey of car owners. It's the biggest customer satisfaction survey of its kind in the UK - based on over 40,000 car owners. The results of the survey made the evening news on national TV, so I guess the public has changed its mind about the quality of central European engineering. But the real indication of our success is the record growth in sales since 1995.

J   The success you've had in dramatically changing the company's image in the UK must give you a great deal of personal satisfaction.

E   Yes, it does. I think I'm very lucky at Skoda. Working with a small team means a lot of personal responsibility. And that's the real enjoyment for me, seeing my ideas having a clear effect on the forward direction of the brand. It's down to me to sort out any problems, so when things go well, I really do feel I'm making an important contribution to the success of the company. And that's an incredibly satisfying feeling.

Unit 5a: Relocation

Listening

A = Amanda   B = Bob

A   Amanda Ramone speaking.
B   Hi, Amanda. It's Bob here.
A   Hi, Bob. Did you get my report about ERS?

B Yeah, no problem. Now, you said you were contacting another company?

A Yeah, I spoke to one this morning, Worldwide Relocation. And they look good.

B And how well do they meet our needs? Do they stand up to ERS?

A They're both pretty similar. Like ERS, they have a house search service ...

B And do they handle all the paperwork? Visas, work permits ...?

A Yeah. No problems there.

B OK, fine. Now what about transport? You know, removal, shipping.

A Let me just ... . Oh right. Here it is. No, this is something Worldwide don't offer.

B Whereas ERS do. Mmm. How do you feel about that, Amanda?

A I don't know, but I don't see this as a major problem. I think it's something you can handle from the Seattle end.

B OK. And what else? How about finding schools?

A Yeah. They have a school search service. And another interesting thing is that they run orientation and cultural integration programmes.

B Mmm. Sounds interesting, Amanda. So what's your feeling on this?

A Well, neither company meets all our key needs, but there's no-one else in the picture.

B And in terms of cost?

A In terms of cost, ERS are offering the best deal. However, cost isn't a major issue here.

B You know, it worries me that ERS offer no partner employment assistance. How about Worldwide?

A Yes, and very successfully. The guy I spoke to said that they can normally arrange employment for the partner within three months. And as most of our people have wives or husbands, ...

B Yeah. That's the main problem for me with ERS.

A For me, too.

B OK, Amanda. Well, you're closest to this. What's your view?

Unit 5b: New premises

Listening 1

G = Gerald   J = Jim

G PLP Immobilier. Bonjour?

J Hello, Gerald? It's Jim Flowers here.

G Hello, Jim. Nice to hear from you. What can I do for you?

J Listen, Gerald. I'm just on my way to have a look at that office site you mentioned the other day.

G Oh, yeah?

J The thing is, I know the street name, but I can't remember where it is exactly. Do you think you could give me directions?

G Yes, of course. Where are you now?

J Well, I've just parked the car and I'm in rue de Tournelles just outside a supermarket.

G Rue de Tournelles? Oh, yes. I know. Now let me see. OK. Right. Now, if you look right, you'll see a bank on the corner. It's called BNP.

J OK. Yes, yes I can see that.

G Right. Well, walk to the bank, to the corner, and that's rue de Balzac. You turn left there and cross over to the other side of the street.

J Right.

G Then take the first road on the right. That's rue de Paradis. Oh, and you'll see a big café on that corner. Keep going along that street until you come to a theatre. I think you'll cross over two or three other streets on the way, but just keep straight on till you reach the theatre.

J Right. OK. So, I take the first right and just keep going straight on until the theatre.

G That's right. Now just before the theatre, on the left, is a small street. You go down there, and about halfway along is a kind of a square, with a statue in the middle.

J Right.

G And it's on the right. It's a big, white modern building. You can't miss it.

J Thanks, Gerald. Speak to you soon.

G Bye, Jim. Oh, and let me know what you think of it.

J Will do.

Listening 2

G = Gerald   J = Jim

G PLP Immobilier. Bonjour?

J Hello, Gerald? It's Jim Flowers again.

G Hello, Jim. So what did you think of the avenue Voltaire site?

J I'm quite interested, Gerald. There are just a few details I'd like to check before we go any further, though.

G OK, Jim. Let me just get the papers out. Right. So what would you like to know?

J Well, first of all, I'd like to know about availability.

G Well, there's a little renovation work being done at the moment, but it should be free for occupation on 1 August.

J Sorry. Sorry, Gerald. I didn't get that. I'm on my mobile. Could you say that again, please?

G Yes, it should be free on 1 August.

J 1 August. Right. That would fit in quite well with our plans. Good. And what about the floors? Which are free at the moment?

G Let me see. It's the fourth, the sixth, and the seventh.

J The fourth ... Sorry. Did you say the fifth?

G No. The fourth, the sixth, and the seventh.

J Right. OK. Thanks. Oh, and can you tell me about car parking facilities? I didn't see a car park at the front.

G Actually, there's quite a large underground car park for the building. It takes over 400 cars. But with public transport being so good, it's usually never more than half full.

J So how many metro stations are there nearby?

G Three. And all of them are less than 10 minutes' walk away.

J Right. That's great for the moment. Do you think you could put something in the post?

G No problem. I'll get something off to you today.

J Thanks a lot. I'll talk to you soon.

Unit 5: Exam practice

Part One

Conversation One

J = Joanna   P = Peter

J Joanna Rivers.

P Hello, Joanna. It's Peter. Is David there?

J No, I'm sorry, Peter. He's just left the office.

P What time will he be back?

J Not till tomorrow, I'm afraid. Can I take a message?

P Yes, OK. It's about a training course he was interested in. Could you tell him the name of the course is 'Managing People', and it's on 13 August?

J OK, so that's 'Managing People' on 13 August.

P Yes, so he'll have to be quick if he's interested. The woman who runs the course is called Virginia Little, and he should call her direct. Her number's 01723 887762.

J OK, Peter. I'll make sure he gets this when he comes in.

P OK, and one other thing. Tell David to mention my name. Virginia's an old friend of mine.

Conversation Two

LT = Longside Taxis   J = James

LT Longside Taxis.

J Morning. This is James Wright from Wentworth Engineering. I'd like to book a taxi, please.

LT You're very busy today. That's the fourth one you've booked this morning!

M I know. We've got a big sales promotion on today.

LT Oh, I see. Right. So when do you want it for?

M Half past four.

LT And the passenger's name, please?

M Roughton, Susan Roughton.

LT Can you spell that?

M Yes, it's R-O-U-G-H-T-O-N.

LT OK. I've got that. And where's she going?

M To the airport.

LT Is that Heathrow or Gatwick?

M Let me just check. It's Gatwick.

LT Right. OK. And where's the pick-up point?

M From here, from the main offices on Milton Road.

LT Will she be waiting at the main reception?

M Yes, that's right.

LT OK. And does this go on your account or is the passenger paying?

M She's paying herself.

LT Right. Thanks a lot.

Conversation Three

S = Stephanie   A = Alan

S Ridgeway Park. Stephanie James speaking.

A Hello, Mrs James. This is Alan Barker, here.

S Oh, hello, Dr Barker. I was going to call you today about your talk next month. It's getting quite close now and there are a couple of things I need to check and finalise with you.

A OK.

S Well, the first thing is the title of your talk. I have here 'Assessing Performance'. But you said you might want to change it.

A Yes, that's right. The new title is now 'Measuring Performance'.

S OK. And I also need to know if you'd prefer to give your talk in our conference room or lecture theatre.

A I'd prefer the conference room, if that's possible.

S That's no problem at all. Most speakers prefer that. And what about equipment? Is there anything special you'll need?

A Well, apart from the usual things like a whiteboard and VCR, I'll need a CD-player.

S I'm afraid we haven't got one. Would a cassette player do instead?

A Yes, that'll ... that'll be OK.

S Right. I'll make a note of that. Oh, and there's one other thing. Can I just confirm your fee? Was it £200?

A Well, the actual figure we agreed on was £250. But my organisation will invoice you for that.

S OK, Dr Barker. That's fine. I'll pass that information on to our Accounts Department. And we look forward to seeing you on the 19th.

Part Two

Section One
Thirteen

Well, it's not really used that often in the office. And when you do need it, you normally can't find it because one of the managers takes it home with him sometimes. I think he uses it as a kind of dictation machine. We've tried to record a couple of presentations with it before, but it didn't really work very well because the sound quality isn't very good.

Fourteen

We recently got a new one that's got hundreds of functions on it. It can sort and staple and do all sorts of other clever things. Of course, only the secretary knows how to do any of these things, so even if we want to do something quite simple like duplicate a two-sided document, we have to ask her. If I try to do it, I just end up wasting lots of paper.

Fifteen

It's the first thing I do when I arrive at the office. I press the playback button before I check the fax and switch on the photocopier. Then I sit down and read the post while I'm listening to the messages. I still can't believe how many people leave messages without a name or number. And the worst thing is, of course, people who don't leave any message at all.

Sixteen

Whenever I tell people that we have one in the office, they're always very impressed. They think the company must do some kind of important, secret business. The truth is our Dispatch Department uses it, not our main office. They collect all our waste paper from the photocopier and printer and use it for packaging.

Seventeen

People say it'll be taken over by e-mail, but I can't see it myself. If I want to send a document to someone or a quick drawing, say, then it's the only real solution. It's quick, easy to use and you don't have to worry about compatibility either. And once or twice it's been a life-saver when the photocopier's broken down.

Section Two
Eighteen

This is the third time I've called about this. It's a complete waste of my time and my staff's time. When we ordered the photocopier from you, you assured us it would be installed by one of your engineers and set up ready for use. Well, all your engineer basically did is plug it in and that was that. And now every time we switch it on, we get a warning message. But we don't know what it means because your man didn't even leave us a copy of the manual.

Nineteen

Before we begin, I've been asked to tell you that Dr Jones has been delayed. That means he won't make it in time for his presentation on 'Dealing with Complaints'. Unfortunately, this means we've had to cancel the session and anyone who signed up for it should now choose between the other two sessions which are running this afternoon. Thank you. And now I'll hand you over to Kate.

Twenty

I'm just ringing to tell you about the positive feedback we've had on the presentation you gave the other day. I really appreciate you stepping in like that at the last moment. I know you were a bit nervous, but I'm very grateful you agreed to do it. And looking at the feedback forms, it seems the only complaint was about the size of the room. So, well done!

Twenty-one

I've checked with the Warehouse Manager and it seems there was a mix-up with the transport documents and your order was somehow sent to Gatwick instead of Heathrow. By the time the driver got back to Heathrow, he'd missed the next flight out. And then there was an announcement cancelling the last flight due to technical problems. Anyway, your order'll be on the first plane tomorrow.

Twenty-two

Hello, David. This is Tina Woodhouse. I was just calling to say I'm actually busy on the 15th, so I won't be able to see you in the morning. In fact, I'll be out all that week. So, I was wondering, rather than delaying things any longer, could we bring everything forward to the 14th? If that's OK for you, perhaps you could call me. My extension's 349.

Part Three

A = Alex   S = Sophie

A Job losses are expected at the Manchester plant of the beauty products manufacturer, Vie Vitale. Sophie Jones has been following the story and is in our Manchester studio. Good morning, Sophie.

S   Good morning, Alex.

A   So, job losses, Sophie? How are things going? We've been hearing reports of up to 300 jobs going.

S   Well, if Vie Vitale does go ahead with restructuring and that includes the disposal of its manufacturing base, then as many as 200 of the 500 jobs here are far from guaranteed.

A   And where exactly will these cuts be made, Sophie?

S   Well, most would almost certainly be in the manufacturing division. This is an area Vie Vitale wants to get out of completely. And if this happens, then it would have serious consequences for jobs in distribution. However, the company wants to focus on its product development, so there's unlikely to be any losses there. At least, that's what the company's saying this morning.

A   So very little good news there. But why should the company suddenly find itself in such a difficult position?

S   Well, the health and beauty retail sector is still as fashionable as ever and has attracted a lot of new companies to the market. The sad truth is, though, that these new companies now have equally good if not better ideas at the same kind of price. And I think this is the fundamental problem. And last year, La Face, the French manufacturer, brought out a new range - again, very similar types of products, very similar sorts of ideas.

A   So how well are La Face doing?

S   Well, actually, they haven't been doing that well either. In fact, only last week they announced they're no longer going to focus on their own retail outlets, but rather on the mail order side of the business instead. They're also considering selling through department stores, but nothing's been confirmed yet. So Vie Vitale isn't alone in feeling incredible pressure.

A   Well, it sounds like the problem they're all having is that it's getting quite crowded. So what does all this mean for Vie Vitale's share price?

S   Well, if we look at the share price over the last year, you can see that although it started high at the beginning of the year and looked steady in the first six months, there's been a huge drop since then, reaching its lowest point last week where the City really lost confidence in what they were doing.

A   Right. Now, Vie Vitale's corporate image used to be unique, didn't it? So how are they planning to establish themselves as the market leader once more?

S   Well, Alex, they're not giving away too many details just yet, but it seems they're intending to freshen up their shops and update their corporate look. You know, all their packaging. There's certainly no news of any new product lines or any change in their basic values.

A   But what about the number of shops? Any change there, Sophie?

S   Well, in fact, what they're doing is buying franchises back. They feel that if they're in control of their shops, they're in control of their corporate image. We've heard nothing about shop closures.

A   So how many of their shops do they now own?

S   Well, they started the process a few months ago and they've now regained control of all their French outlets. And they should have ownership of all their German shops by early next year. As there are more outlets in the UK, it'll take a bit longer here. I think the name of the game is definitely going to be control.

> **Exam focus: Speaking Test contains a mock oral test. No tapescript is provided.**

Unit 6a: Reporting results

Listening

●   So, let's have a look at how the markets are doing with Jenny.

▼   Thanks, Tony. Well, we'll begin with Budgens, the supermarket chain. They've reported their results today. For the six months, pre-tax profits rose sharply by 9.8%, which brought the final figure for the year to just over 6.3m. That's up from just over 5.8m last year. The dividend is up. If you're one of their shareholders, you can expect half a penny per share. Budgens has got 163 stores and three now actually sell petrol, so they do seem to be expanding. They've also just spent half a million pounds on buying something called TeleShop Services, which specialises in developing computer-based home shopping. However, the business is only operating at break-even and isn't expected to do much more this year, it has to be said.

Now, let's take a look, shall we, at how Budgens' share price has done over the last 12 months. As you can see, it's been pretty volatile. After steady progress throughout the first half of the year, it really shot up at the end of the summer, when everyone thought there'd be a takeover. At the height of the rumours, in September, you can see that shares peaked at just over 80 pence. The takeover didn't happen, though, and the price collapsed. By mid-October it had fallen as far as the 55 pence mark. The shares recovered slowly to 65 pence by November, but then they went into steady decline again for the next two months, down once again to the 55 pence mark. However, news of good trading results has meant that shares have improved again this year. And it has to be said, the share price is marginally up on last February, so shareholders are in profit over the 12 month period. And if we look at the Budgens shares today, they're up slightly by 1.3 pence at 67 and a half.

Unit 6b: Environmental report

Listening

Good morning. Today we're going to look at ICI's environmental programmes and environmental performance since 1990. I'd like to begin with some background to ICI's environmental projects. Then we'll go on to look at our Challenge 2000 project. And finally, we'll turn to the results of these programmes.

Now, the story really begins in the 1980s when people started becoming more concerned about environmental issues. The first ICI environmental project was a result of the realisation that, as a major player in the chemicals industry, ICI would have to address these growing public concerns. So, in 1990 we presented our shareholders with a programme to reduce the environmental impact of our worldwide activities. Many of the steps we took back then have since become government legislation. The project included some very ambitious targets for improving the company's environmental performance. We realised that these goals demanded significant investment, so we committed the largest share of our annual £500 million Safety, Health and Environment budget to the project. Since 1990 we've spent about 200 million each year on environmental improvements. As things developed, we soon realised that there were no cheap options or quick fixes. Therefore, we began directing this expenditure to the biggest problems, where solutions would bring the biggest improvements. And then, in 1995, we assessed our performance and set ourselves equally demanding objectives for the next five years. These formed the basis of our Challenge 2000 project.

If you'd like to look at the screen, you'll see the four main objectives of Challenge 2000. As you can see, our first objective is to ensure that by the year 2000 all our businesses comply with the relevant environmental regulations in each of the countries in which their products are sold. This applies to all our new and existing plants throughout the world. Our second objective is to improve energy efficiency. Now, here, we decided that by the year 2000 we would reduce our energy consumption by 10%. The starting point for this reduction would be the 1995 level. Moving on to the next objective, ICI intends to halve the environmental impact of its businesses by the year 2000. I'm sure you'll understand exactly how ambitious this is, but we feel it demonstrates the importance of the issue. To achieve this target, we decided to concentrate on those wastes which pose the greatest threat to the environment and give their reduction the highest priority. And finally, our last objective is to ensure that all our businesses have what we call Product Stewardship Programmes. These programmes are a tool for managing all our chemicals throughout their complete product life cycle. They'll provide up-to-date records of all the chemicals that we use and handle. And what's more, they'll ensure that all labels and public information are printed in the languages of our customers. The results of these programmes will be published each year in a special report.

Now, it's clear that growing public concern about the future of the environment will affect government thinking - and no-one in the industry doubts that tougher legislation is to come. That's why Challenge 2000 is such an essential part of ICI's strategic development. With the improvements we're making today, we can feel confident about fulfilling the legal obligations of tomorrow. At ICI we realise that we have a commitment not only to our customers, employees and shareholders, but also to the communities in which we work and produce our goods.

So now I'd like to turn to the results of the ...

Unit 7a: Health and safety

Listening

N = Nurse   P = Peter

N   OK. Let me have a look at it. Yes, that looks nasty. So how did it happen?
P   Well, it's stupid really. I was trying to fix the light in my office.
N   But that's a job for maintenance.
P   I know. But I told them about it days ago and nothing happened. So I thought I'd try.
N   Well, you really must be more careful. There are very strict guidelines here about that kind of thing. And if you have an accident, the company doesn't have to accept responsibility, you know?
P   I know. But the light kept going on and off all day. It was driving me crazy.
N   So what happened? Did you fall?
P   Well, I couldn't reach the light. So I climbed onto my desk, and then I lost my balance and fell.
N   And you banged your head?
P   Ouch! Yes. I caught it on the edge of a filing cabinet.
N   Do you feel sick or dizzy?
P   No, but it really is hurting a lot now. Will I need any stitches, do you think?
N   No, no, it's quite a small cut really, I'll just clean and dress it. We needn't bother about stitches. But it is a nasty bump, though. Are you taking any medication at the moment?
P   No.
N   Right. Here are some painkillers. Take two of these three times a day for the next two or three days. But you mustn't drink alcohol while you're taking them.
P   OK.
N   And pop in tomorrow some time and I'll have another look at it.
P   Thanks. See you tomorrow.

Unit 7b: Rights at work

Listening

1   I didn't really feel I was abusing the system. I mean everybody does it. It was just a few small things really - a fax here, a few photocopies there. I felt it was justified. After all, I did do a lot of unpaid overtime and I took work home with me. They seemed really pleased with my performance, so I honestly didn't think they'd mind.

2   My boss didn't mind if I arrived a couple of minutes late in the mornings but if I wanted to leave on time, well that was a completely different story. Well, after six months, I'd just had enough of it, working late every day of the week. So one day I told him straight: I'd only work the hours I'd agreed in my contract.

3   I was having problems because I just couldn't seem to prioritise my work and organise my time. So I suppose it looked to my boss as if I couldn't do the job. But it's ridiculous really. I could do it, but I just couldn't seem to keep up with the workload. And this was a place where results were everything.

4   I knew my turn would come soon. But I hated the whole idea of spending three hours in the car every day just getting to work and back. It was OK for some of the others, I mean, they lived nearer the new site. But if I'd had to work overtime, I'd never have got home before 9 o'clock. Well, in the end, I just couldn't do it. And I wouldn't do it. And that's what I told them.

5   I suppose they didn't want to carry me any longer. I think people just got fed up with having to cover for me and take on all my work when I was away. But it seems a pretty poor show to sack someone for something that isn't their fault. I mean, no-one wants to be ill, do they?

Unit 8a: Business expenses

Listening 1

Conversation 1
D = David   R = Roger

D   David Hobbs.
R   Hello, Mr Hobbs. This is Roger Hargreaves from Accounts. I'm just ringing about your expenses claim. There are a couple of things I need to check.
D   OK. What do you need to know?
R   Well, you put down that it was a business trip. But do you think you could be a bit more specific?
D   Yes, sorry. It was actually a marketing conference.
R   OK. And you stayed at the Cartlands Hotel. But you didn't put down how much it cost.
D   Oh, sorry. It was £80. And that was for one night.
R   I see. Now under 'Client Entertaining' you put £56.70 for a meal and drinks. But you are supposed to put down the name of anybody you entertain, you know.
D   I'm sorry. I must have forgotten. Anyway, the client's name is Limbert. Paul Limbert. He's one of our Belgian suppliers.
R   Could you spell his last name for me?
D   Limbert? Yes, it's L-I-M-B-E-R-T.
R   Right, thanks. Oh, and this amount for £9.00 under 'Other Expenses'. What exactly was that for?
D   £9.00? Let me see. £9.00? Oh, yes. That was for a couple of faxes I had to send from the hotel.

Conversation 2
A = Alison   R = Roger

A   Alison Forbes.
R   Hello, Alison. It's Roger Hargreaves from Accounts. Is Alan there, please?
A   I'm afraid he isn't in today. Can I help at all?
R   I don't think so, no. It's about his expenses, you know, for the trip to Sweden.
A   Can I give him a message?
R   Yes, if you could. Could you tell him that something was missing? It was his hotel bill. And I need it quickly if he wants us to pay him this month.
A   Actually, I think he was looking for it the other day.

R   *I hope he hasn't lost it. Well, look, if he can't find it, he really needs to call me as soon as possible.*
A   *OK. I'll tell him.*
R   *Thanks. Oh, and one other thing. The last time we paid him his expenses, he asked us to pay him in cash. Well, I'm afraid it caused all kinds of problems, and everyone started asking for cash payments. So we've decided that we really can't do that again.*
A   *OK, I'll let him know. Bye.*

Conversation 3

C = Chris   R = Roger

C   *Hello?*
R   *Hello, Mr Evans?*
C   *Speaking.*
R   *This is Roger Hargreaves. I'm just ringing about your expenses for the Paris trip.*
C   *Well, you do know I lost my case on that trip? So I'm afraid I can't give you any receipts or anything.*
R   *That's not a problem. I just need to check a few details.*
C   *OK. What do you need to know?*
R   *Well, first of all, when was the trip exactly?*
C   *Let me just check my diary. Yes, it was the last weekend in June. The 25th and 26th.*
R   *So one night. Right. And where did you stay?*
C   *Hotel Continental. But I'm afraid I can't remember the price. But it's the same hotel I stayed at last time. In fact, it was even the same room.*
R   *Fine. I can look that up. And what about travel? Did you fly or take the train?*
C   *The train. Eurostar. But, again, I can't remember the price.*
R   *That's OK. I can check it myself. Oh, and were there any other expenses?*
C   *I can't think of anything. Oh, yes there was actually. I had to buy metro tickets to get around Paris.*
R   *Metro tickets ... that would be about £5, wouldn't it?*
C   *That sounds about right.*
R   *OK, Mr Evans, thanks very much.*

Listening 2

1   *Good morning. This is a message for David Eastman. I got your note about my expenses form - about returning it to you. Well, actually I did send it to you. The only problem is it went to the wrong department, and that's why you still haven't got it. Anyway, I'll bring it round first thing in the morning, OK? Oh, sorry, this is Alex Eddington, by the way.*

2   *Hello, this is June Salisbury. You wanted to speak to me about my expenses claim for the Munich trip. Could we get together on Friday morning to talk about it? Perhaps at about 11, if that's all right? Just give my secretary a call. OK. Bye.*

3   *This is Bob Richards here. Listen, I've just found another receipt for my Oslo trip last month. It's for quite a lot of photocopies I had done in a shop. I suppose it's too late for this month, but is it OK if I put this through on next month's expenses? Could you get back to me and let me know? OK. Bye.*

4   *Hello, this is Patricia Graves from Sales. Look, I'm ringing about my expenses again. The last time I called you, you said they'd be included in this month's pay. Well, I've checked with my bank and they're not. I can't keep chasing you about this and I'm getting pretty fed up waiting. I'll call by your office sometime tomorrow, and this time, I'd like a cheque. Goodbye.*

5   *Hello, David. This is Simon. Look, about this morning, I'm afraid something urgent's come up and I have to rush off to London, so I won't be able to make it. I'm really sorry it's such short notice. I'll call you when I get back. OK? Speak to you soon.*

Unit 8b: Business travel

Listening

1   *Any regular business traveller will tell you how important this is if you want to feel ready to face a whole day of business meetings. Sometimes, you work straight through meal-times, so it might be the only thing you'll get until you step on the plane for your flight home. And who wants to have to start looking for a burger bar at midnight?*

2   *From the business traveller's point of view, flexibility and choice are absolutely crucial. Businesses can't depend on airlines offering a flight on a particular day or time of their choosing. I really do feel that getting to and from your destination at a time which suits you and fits in with your plans is essential, and one of the main reasons for choosing an airline.*

3   *I just find it really annoying. After I've eaten, I just want to sit quietly, have a drink and read my newspaper. The last thing I want is to listen to people screaming with laughter at some ridiculous comedy.*

4   *On a short trip, it's not so important. You're not there long enough to have more than a drink and a quick look at the paper. But on a long trip, you really need to be able to stretch out, lie back and get some proper sleep.*

5   *Of course, I could get a cheaper seat, but that's not the point. With a long day of meetings and negotiations ahead of me, I need a bit of comfort and looking after, and my company understands that. It's also a good place for networking, and I've often got into conversation with the person next to me, who's developed into a useful contact.*

Unit 9a: Flexible benefits

Listening

I = Interviewer   D = David Thompson

I   *Maybe you'd like to begin by explaining how Choices came about.*
D   *Well, we wanted to show that PricewaterhouseCoopers recognised the individuality and diversity of all its employees. Flexible benefits was the ideal way of sending this message without massively increasing the firm's payroll costs. Also, after the merger between the two firms, Price Waterhouse and Coopers & Lybrand, we wanted a new scheme that both sets of employees could identify with.*
I   *And what advantages does Choices give employees?*
D   *Well, it sounds obvious, but the main advantage is choice and the opportunity to change benefits as an employee's lifestyle changes. There's also a price advantage on many of the benefits.*
I   *How does that work?*
D   *Well, there are tax savings when taking certain benefits rather than cash. But the real advantage is that our size means that we can find the best providers in the market and then negotiate bulk discounts with them.*
I   *And how did you inform employees of all this when you launched the scheme?*
D   *We had to be very pro-active to ensure employees understood everything about Choices, from its concept to its implementation. We began by creating awareness with printed material, and then ran a series of countrywide roadshows.*
I   *Roadshows? Why did you choose roadshows?*
D   *Because they were the ideal way of offering employees a face-to-face opportunity to develop their understanding of Choices and get the answers they needed. People were already going through huge changes with the merger, so we had to expect some challenging questions.*
I   *And how successful were the roadshows?*

D   Well, they were attended by 8,000 out of 19,000 UK employees. And since then, research among staff has shown very high awareness levels and a very good understanding of why Choices was introduced.

I   And where did you go from there?

D   Well, having created awareness and interest, we then had to encourage employee participation. We did this by making detailed information about Choices available to all employees electronically. Any employees needing further information could then contact the Choices call centre if they needed to.

I   From the feedback you've had so far, which benefits do you think will prove most popular?

D   Well, we don't know yet. But things like pensions and company cars are likely to prove popular. But typically, with flexible benefits, most interest is shown in varying the amount of annual leave. And I expect it'll be the same with Choices.

I   You mean people taking more days off?

D   Well, not just more. Many employees actually reduce their annual allowance in exchange for cash. It's just another example of the flexibility which characterises Choices - which, as we know from post-recruitment interviews, can be a real factor when people are comparing job offers.

I   Yes, I can imagine. Choices must have had a real effect on recruitment.

D   Well, it only went live in April, so it's still too early to say exactly what effect it's going to have. But with Flex, the old benefits scheme that Price Waterhouse used to have before the merger, there was a 30% increase in the number of candidates who accepted job offers. We expect Choices to be just as effective, and help us get the brightest and the best - both university graduates and experienced applicants.

I   And finally, what do you see as the main benefit for PricewaterhouseCoopers?

D   Well, for one thing, it should reduce staff turnover. Replacing an employee through an agency can be a very expensive business. But most importantly, it'll help define the PricewaterhouseCoopers image and send a clear signal about our values to employees and job applicants. There's also the experience it gives us in running flexible benefits schemes.

I   What do you mean exactly?

D   Well, flexible benefits is something our consultancy service is asked to advise companies on. So Choices provides us with invaluable experience.

Unit 9b: Staff appraisal

Listening

1   We spoke about how things were going in general and then we finally got down to discussing my workload. We talked about how we could define my duties more clearly and she agreed that I could hand over some of my work to colleagues. So, hopefully, I'll now be able to concentrate on the things I was hired to do in the first place.

2   My boss said that even though money was tight, they'd support me if I wanted to study for a management qualification. She said that the company could subsidise the cost of the course, and she promised to be flexible about holidays. But the company would benefit from the skills I'd learn anyway, so it's in their interests as well.

3   It was very difficult because the company's been quite good to me, really. I mean, the conditions are good and I can't really complain about salary, either. But I explained I'd been here five years now and I'm still doing the same job. I also mentioned that I'd applied for a couple of internal vacancies but got nowhere. And on one occasion the position was given to someone who started well after I did.

4   Well, it started off with the usual stuff. You know, he thanked me for all the hard work and things like that. But then he started on about missed deadlines and careless mistakes. The thing is, half of the things he mentioned weren't even my responsibility. I complained about the lack of support I'd had from management but he just wasn't interested. And then he asked me to write a full report on what had gone wrong. I couldn't believe it!

5   All in all, the appraisal was very positive. The only thing is, of course, having such a successful year means that management gets carried away and expects miracles from you all the time. I told my boss that I wasn't sure we'd be able to repeat last year's performance. But he ignored me, of course, and produced this set of ridiculous objectives that he thought'd be an 'exciting challenge'. You really have to wonder sometimes which planet management's on.

Unit 10a: Marketing disasters

Listening

1   It was my idea in the first place, and it did give us really catchy slogans like, 'When you see this offer, you'll think you're seeing double'. But what happened was a chance in a million, and they'd all come by car! So what could I do? If we'd cancelled the promotion, it would have caused a riot. In the end, it cost the company thousands - and it cost me my job.

2   In theory, it was a brilliant idea, but I don't think anyone ever imagined it would attract so much interest. Looking back, I suppose it was bound to with big prize money like that. It wouldn't have been so bad if the questions had been more difficult. That was probably our biggest mistake. Some of them were so easy, even my seven-year-old was able to find the answers. But the whole thing was a catalogue of disasters from start to finish, really.

3   It's easy to look back now and say we should have done this or that, but at the time, well ... I suppose it would've been OK if we hadn't allowed flat-owners to enter, but with a big promotion you don't want to exclude anyone. In the end, we offered the winner money instead and tried to keep it as quiet as we could. If we'd taken any publicity photos, we would have looked ridiculous.

Unit 10b: Going global

Listening

I = Interviewer   D = Donald

I   Donald, your consultancy helps companies enter foreign markets. What kind of help are companies looking for when they come to KMP?

D   Well, companies usually have a specific market in mind and a pretty good idea as to which products they intend to export. But what they're not sure about is how to get the product into the target market.

I   So what is the best way?

D   Well, there are many options, from franchises to wholly-owned subsidiaries. The higher the degree of ownership, the more control you have. However, ownership also means more investment and, therefore, more risk.

I   So what's the safest way of entering a market?

D   Well, if you want to keep financial risk to a minimum, you should think about a licensing arrangement or perhaps a franchise. That way you don't have any of the costs associated with setting up production facilities. And, of course, you retain control of the product, which means you avoid some of the conflicts involved in joint ventures.

I   But joint ventures are a very popular way of entering foreign markets.

D   Yes, they are, because they allow a company to share some of the costs and risk. And even more importantly, they provide essential local knowledge without the cost of having to acquire a company. But *they're not risk-free.*

I   So, what are the dangers of joint ventures?

D   Well, in a typical joint venture the two partners pool their know-how and learn from each other as they work together. But, in fact, it's actually a learning race. One firm might learn much faster than the other and start taking all the decisions. It could eventually decide it has no more use for the arrangement and even terminate it.

I   So, if you wanted to keep control and avoid that, a wholly-owned subsidiary would be the best option, then?

D   It really depends on the target market. If, say, there's potentially a very high demand, then it would make sense to buy or set up a subsidiary and produce locally, because of economies of scale. Distance, of course, is another factor. Shipping to the other side of the world can be very expensive. That's why a lot of Japanese companies produce in Europe.

I   And what other factors can improve a company's chance of success?

D   Well, as I said, our clients usually know which products they want to export, but they often don't realise how much their product needs to be adapted. You see, some products require an understanding of local needs and an ability to use this knowledge in the product's design.

I   OK. So, let's say a company has successfully entered a market. How quickly should it look to expand?

D   Well, once again, it's finding the best way of minimising risk while optimising opportunity. However, under certain circumstances, a company is forced to expand in order to survive.

I   And when is this the case?

D   When, for example, you enter a market with a successful formula that's easy to copy - because you'll soon have a lot of local competitors offering the same products or services. Now, unless you're in a position to expand quickly enough to make economies of scale possible, these local companies will soon undercut you and price you out of the market.

I   And how can a company prepare for this expansion?

D   Well, the key to expansion is not spreading your managerial and financial resources too thinly. That's why it's crucial to develop a long-term strategy and make a thorough assessment of all the resources available for expansion. Otherwise, you won't be able to defend and profit from the market presence you've created.

Unit 10: Exam practice

Part One

Conversation One
IBS = Initial Business Supplies   LG = Lacey Graphics

IBS   Initial Business Supplies. Good morning.

LG   Good morning. This is Lacey Graphics. I'd like to place an order, please.

IBS   OK. I'll just get an order form. Right. Now, it's Lacey Graphics?

LG   That's right. We have an account with you.

IBS   Sorry. I didn't know. I'm new here.

LG   Oh, that's OK.

IBS   Could you give me your address, please?

LG   Yes, of course. It's Unit 5, Hailsham Industrial Estate, Hailsham.

IBS   And that's the delivery address?

LG   Yes.

IBS   And could I have your name, please?

LG   Well, I'm Liz Price, but I'd like you to address it to the 'Office Manager', please.

IBS   OK. Fine. Now what's the order for?

LG   We'd like 10 boxes of printer paper.

IBS   I'm afraid we haven't got any printer paper at the moment. Will photocopy paper do?

LG   Yes, that'll be fine.

IBS   And when would you like it?

LG   Well, as soon as possible, really. We've nearly run out.

IBS   I can get it to you on Thursday, if you like.

LG   That's great. Thanks.

IBS   And how will you be paying?

LG   Well, you usually send us an invoice.

IBS   OK. And that's to the same address?

LG   That's right.

Conversation Two
S = Sarah   D = David

S   Hello, David. It's Sarah.

D   Hello, Sarah.

S   David, I'm just going over my notes for the advertisement we're putting in the paper. There are still one or two bits of information I need.

D   OK. What do you need to know?

S   Well, you still haven't given me the final job title yet.

D   Oh, sorry. The job title should be 'Regional Manager'.

S   And what salary should I put?

D   Well, it depends on the quality of the candidate, really. Just put 'competitive salary plus benefits'. What we'll ask them to do is send details of their current salary and we'll go from there.

S   So you want me to put that in the advert as well?

D   Yes. Add it to the bit about applicants including their CVs and references.

S   OK. And have you decided when you'll be holding interviews?

D   Yes. It'll be the last week in April. So that's, what, the week starting the 25th?

S   No, I think its the 26th, actually.

D   OK.

S   And you gave me a date of 17 March. That's the closing date for applications?

D   That's right.

S   Right, David. I think that's everything. Thanks.

Conversation Three
A = Anna   R = Roger

A   Simpson & Co. Good morning.

R   Hello, Anna?

A   Oh, hello Roger.

R   I'm glad I caught you. Listen, I'm at the airport, and I've just realised I've left my diary in the office. You can't see it anywhere, can you?

A   Hang on. Here it is.

R   Oh, great. Now can you have a look at tomorrow? I've got an appointment at eleven-thirty at Maplo. But what's the name of the woman I'm seeing?

A   It's Delorme. Marie Delorme.

R   That's it. It had gone right out of my head. Is that D-E-L-O-R-M-E?

A   That's right.

R   And what's her position in the company, exactly?

A   She's their new Research Director.

R   That's it. Right. Then in the afternoon, I'm meeting Monsieur Belois at 3.30. But I can't remember whether we agreed to meet at his company or the hotel.

A   Well, there's nothing here about the hotel.

R   Right, then it must be at his company. Sorry, Anna, I'll have to go. My plane's boarding.

A   OK, Roger. Oh, before you go. Don't forget on Friday you'll need to confirm your flight to Rome.

R   Thanks. I'll make a note of it. I'll call you first thing in the morning.

A   Bye.

Part Two

Section One

Thirteen

So, two of the boxes were damaged. And they were the ones with the A3 paper in them. I'm afraid we don't have any more of that in stock. But we've got a delivery coming tomorrow. So we'll send you two new boxes as soon as we can, if that's OK.

Fourteen

Well, if you can wait a while, there's something coming up in the next few weeks. Now I haven't seen it myself, but I've been told by the owners that it should be ready for immediate occupation. So, as long as you can work out the finance and insurance in time, you should be in by the start of next month. And it's a lot cheaper than the other site you were considering.

Fifteen

Yes, we can arrange it now, if you'd like, if you want to pay by credit card. And if time's the most important factor, then that's what I'd recommend. That way, we can guarantee it'll arrive by 8.30 tomorrow morning. But somebody will have to sign for it, of course.

Sixteen

The way it works is that we negotiate an agreed limit with you, say £400. Now if you use this facility, there's a flat monthly charge of £5, and then there's the interest on the overdraft as well, of course, which is 17.5% at the moment. If you do find that this amount doesn't meet your needs, you can always come in and we can look at the situation again.

Seventeen

You can organise your insurance through us - against accidents, theft and loss of baggage for the duration of the trip. We use Non-Stop, a leading company in the business. We find their rates very competitive. So, for two weeks that'll be £34. Shall I just add the premium on to the fare?

Section Two

Eighteen

Hello. This is Arkwright Engineering and I'm calling on behalf of James Peterson. Mr Peterson would like to thank you for your letter, and would be delighted to attend the Frankfurt fair as your guest. He's away in Helsinki until the end of the week, but he'll contact you on his return to finalise arrangements.

Nineteen

Good morning. My name's Helen Cooper. I was wondering if there are any places still available for the 'Managers in the Millennium' workshop in Manchester in November. Actually, I wanted to do the same workshop in December - but it was cancelled. If there are any places free, could you please call me on 0181 5327391? Thanks.

Twenty

Hi. It's Petra here. I've heard you've been having problems with your computer and it's refusing to print again. Do you want me to come and have a look at it? I've got an appointment at five but should be free after six.

Twenty-one

Hello. It's Paul Sinclair from Sasspro again. Look, I'm sorry to bother you - but when I called earlier, I'm afraid I was working from an old set of figures. We actually need four thousand copies of the brochure not three thousand. I'd be grateful if you could give me a quick call just to confirm this figure. Thanks a lot. Bye.

Twenty-two

Good morning. This is Peter Williams. I'm afraid a very serious problem has come up here and I've got to stay and deal with it tomorrow. So this means that I can't make our meeting. It'd be great if we could get together later in the week some time. Could you give me a ring to confirm that you've got this message? Thanks.

Part Three

P = Presenter   J = Jim

P Good morning, Mr Hayes.

J Good morning.

P Now, Mr Hayes. Do we really need to be concerned about health and safety standards in the workplace? I thought things were improving. Surely they can't be worse?

J On the whole, I'd certainly agree with you. Clearly things have moved on a great deal in recent years. But that really isn't the issue here.

P So what exactly is the issue?

J Well, quite simply, the seriousness of health and safety offences is no longer reflected in the fines handed out to companies.

P So, in other words, you'd like to see fines increased. But how high would you like to see them go?

J Well, at the moment, the maximum fine which can be imposed by a Magistrates Court is £20,000. What the Health and Safety Commission has been pushing for for a very long time is unlimited fines.

P Which at the moment only the Crown Court can hand out.

J Exactly, yes. We'd like to see a lot more cases going to the Crown Court. And this is an area where we've been pushing for government and union support.

P But Mr Hayes, I can't really imagine that you want to put companies out of business with massive fines.

J Well, in extreme cases, that's exactly what we do want. When the offence is so serious that an employee has been killed, for example, then the employer really shouldn't stay in business. Look, the real purpose of the higher fines isn't necessarily to punish offenders but to make other companies think very carefully about their own health and safety practices.

P You mean make examples of offenders?

J Well, you could say that, yes. But you must remember there are established codes of practice. By ignoring them, employers are making the workplace unsafe. And quite simply they're breaking the law.

P So, a heavy fine for a big, high-profile company would be an ideal way of generating maximum publicity for your commission?

J Well, it would have that effect, yes. But that's not the way it works. While ability to pay can, on occasion, be taken into account, the size of the fines should reflect the level of neglect shown by the employer.

P Right. Now just how successful are local authorities when they take action against companies who break health and safety regulations?

J Well, apart from a few cases, local authority prosecutions are generally very successful.

P Well that sounds pretty encouraging, Mr Hayes.

J But not so encouraging when you consider that the average penalty in nearly 1,000 cases last year was only about £1,500. Now, many companies spend more than £2,000 on photocopies alone each month. What we must have is a level of fine which will shock them into action.

P And yet, as you said earlier, health and safety standards are improving. And I believe the number of cases against companies has actually fallen slightly in each of the last four years.

J Oh, that's correct. And I think it's clear companies are focusing increased attention on the prevention of accidents. But what hasn't changed is the fact that too many people are still being killed and injured in the workplace each year.

Essential vocabulary

1a: Teamwork

Teamwork
- to allocate (roles)
- to contribute/make a contribution
- to co-operate
- project team
- to take on (responsibility)
- team-building
- team member
- to trust

Training
- to agree on (objectives)
- benefit
- to bring in (a consultant)
- to come up with (ideas)
- to measure (progress)
- seminar
- to set (targets)
- survival course
- to work on (managerial skills)
- to work towards (objectives)

General
- advertisement
- attitude
- effective
- expatriate
- honest
- to make (arrangements)
- to put on (an event)
- schedule
- subsidiary
- under pressure

1b: Communication

Arrangements
- asap (as soon as possible)
- to cancel (a meeting)
- to confirm (arrangements)
- deadline
- to postpone (a meeting)
- to put back (a meeting)

Telephone phrases
- Can I take a message?
- Could I ask who's calling?
- Could I speak to ...?
- Could you get back to me?
- Could you spell that, please?
- I'll ask her to call you
- I'll give him the message
- I'll put you through
- I'm afraid she's not here
- I'm ringing about ...
- Thanks for calling
- This is ...

General
- to adapt
- answering machine
- complimentary (tickets)
- to decline
- native speaker
- to raise (awareness)
- to raise (your voice)
- to return a call
- sensitive
- to simplify (your language)
- trade fair
- voice mail

2a: Entertaining a client

Restaurants
- atmosphere
- bill
- to cater for
- cleanliness
- comfort(able)
- location
- menu
- party (i.e. group of people)
- poor (service)
- speed (of service)
- value for money
- vegetarian

General
- corporate event
- colleague
- criteria
- to entertain
- entertainment
- to launch (a product)
- memorable
- to miss (a flight)
- negotiation
- questionnaire
- to satisfy
- satisfaction
- satisfactory
- wallet

2b: Corporate hospitality

Entertaining
- accommodation
- to chat
- to establish/build (a relationship)
- fact-finding mission
- to get down (to business)
- to meet (expenses)
- round (of golf)
- shopping trip
- sightseeing tour
- sociable
- social setting
- sports event
- (poor) timing
- valued customer

General
- to bring up (a subject)
- contract
- convenient
- delighted
- to finalise (details)
- golden rule
- grateful
- I look forward to ...
- to miss (an opportunity)
- personal assistant (PA)
- to place (an order)
- purpose(ful)
- to set (objectives)
- substantial
- suitable

3a: Ordering goods

Suppliers
- article
- buyer
- to cancel (an order)
- cancellation
- to confirm (an order)
- confirmation
- delivery
- goods
- mail order
- to order
- piece
- quantity
- to recommend
- stock
- to supply
- supplier
- vendor

Catalogues
- catalogue
- collection
- length
- measurement
- to shorten
- standard
- to standardise

General
- headquarters
- to knit
- to reduce
- skirt

3b: Cash flow

Finance
- cash flow
- inflow
- outflow
- cash on delivery
- credit terms
- down payment
- early settlement discount
- to finance
- financing costs
- interest
- labour costs
- (profit) margin
- net
- order book
- outstanding balance
- over-trading
- (late) payment
- penalty charges
- sales price
- turnover
- wages

General
- bar chart
- to benefit
- case study
- components
- to install
- installation
- inventory
- shortage

4a: Brand power

Brands

brand loyalty
brandstretching
competitive advantage
cut-price (goods)
to damage (a brand)
to diversify
diversification
loyalty scheme
own-label (products)
reputation
target customer

General

to attract (customers)
banking sector
to boost (profits)
commitment
credit card
to encourage
growth
incentive
interest rate
mortgage
overheads
performance
personal loan
reliability
saturated
strength
supermarket chain
user-friendliness

4b: Public relations

Marketing and public relations

advertising campaign
company values
to deal with (the press)
display
image
independent opinion
to maintain (goodwill)
(to meet/satisfy) needs
PR (public relations)
press coverage
product launch
reputable
strategy
(to build) understanding

General

to attend (a launch)
availability
to brief (staff)
to finalise (the details)
manufacturing facility/plant
to monitor (replies)
powerful
responsibility
to solve (a problem)
survey
venue

5a: Relocation

Relocating

assistance
brochure
financial aid
to fulfil (needs)
grant
highly efficient
highly sophisticated
infrastructure
investment
network (road/rail/telephone)
overheads
quality of life
rate of inflation
to relocate
removal
running costs
savings
to set up (business)
shipping
work permit

General

aim
to assess
attractive
to compare (favourably with ...)
to conclude
to search
state-of-the-art
tariff

5b: New premises

Describing premises

(easy) access
air conditioning
amenities
boardroom
facilities
floor
immediate (area)
to lease
leasehold/freehold
lift
office site
office space
premises
property
public transport
reception area
renovation
to rent
to share (a building)
square metre (m²)
tenant

General

cross over ...
keep straight on
you can't miss it
appointment
fast-growing
impressive
major
numerous
(wide) range

6a: Reporting results

Describing performance

acquisition
annual report
assets
chairman's statement
cost-cutting (measures)
disposal
dividend
merger
to offset
to restructure
revenue
rumour
sales volume
share price
to streamline
trading results
trading volume

Describing trends

collapse/to collapse
fall/to fall
improvement/to improve
peak/to peak
recovery/to recover
rise/to rise
sharp(ly)
to shoot up
steady/steadily

6b: Environmental report

Environmental impact

by-product
to comply with (regulations)
energy consumption
energy-efficient
environmental impact
environmental issues
environmental legislation
environmental programme
to fulfil (an obligation)
guidelines
hazardous/non-hazardous
to meet (regulations)
priority
product life cycle
to recycle
subsidy
to subsidise
(to reach) a target
to threaten
(to pose) a threat
waste

General

to address (a problem/concern)
to affect
challenge
to focus on
to halve
to realise
to recognise
shareholder

7a: Health and safety

Health and safety

absent (from work)
accident
to arise
cause for concern
findings
first aid
to handle
to harm/to cause harm
to hurt
incident
injury
law
liability
to lift
to lose your balance
painkillers
(to take) precautions
to prevent
reasonable
to require
to review
to revise
risk
to slip
stitches
to strike
to take into account
to trip
workplace

8a: Business expenses

Expenses

amount
to authorise
business trip
to claim/claim back (expenses)
claimant
to come to (£125)
to fill in (a form)
to incur (expenses)
line manager
to make a (false) claim
on business
to process (a claim)
random check
receipt
to reimburse
small print

General

to automate
component
disappointment
frustration
guilt
relief
short notice
urgent
worry

9a: Flexible benefits

Benefits

annual leave
childcare vouchers
company car
health/medical insurance
life assurance
to operate (a system)
pension scheme
retail vouchers
reward
to run (a scheme)
travel insurance

General

applicant
bargaining power
bulk discount
challenging
diversity
graduate
to implement
lump sum
optional
payroll
provider
recruitment
security
staff turnover

7b: Rights at work

Rights at work

to abuse (a system)
to ban
to be allowed to
case
to deal with (complaints)
to dismiss/sack (an employee)
to draw up/formulate (a policy)
grievance
industrial tribunal
to keep up with (work)
(to know your) rights
to meet (a target)
to observe (regulations)
plaintiff
to put up with (a disturbance)
sexual harassment
unfair dismissal
verbal/written warning
workload
to work overtime

General

to behave
to consult
to commute
to exaggerate
to face
to lie
to negotiate
to prioritise

8b: Business travel

Air travel

air miles
baggage allowance
business class
check-in
delay
duty-free
frequent flyer
in-flight (catering)
legroom
lounge
on-board (entertainment)
priority status
reclining (seat)
scheduled flight
take-off
to transfer

General

to annoy
to bear
to compete with (other companies)
to fail
frills
low-cost
mainstream
privacy
refreshment
to refund
to select
to survive
to undercut (competitors)

9b: Staff appraisal

Appraisals

to appraise (employees)
to comment on (performance)
to co-ordinate (goals)
to criticise
to evaluate (performance)
(to give/get) feedback
job description
to meet (aims/objectives/deadlines)
to miss (targets/deadlines)
(training) policy
to praise
promotion
prospects

General

to cause (concern)
corporate strategy
current
to define (duties/roles)
to ensure (success)
to fail (to respond)
to hire
to ignore
instance
internal vacancy
noticeboard
(good/bad) practice
qualification

Essential vocabulary

Essential functions

10a: Marketing disasters

Marketing

at the bottom end (of the market)
to attract (interest)
marketing mix
to position (a product)
promotion
promotional gift
research
rival
to run (a competition)
top-of-the-range
to win (market share)
to win (a prize)
to withdraw (a product)

General

to avoid (mistakes/disasters)
clue
to coincide with
confectionery
conservatory
flawed
to go into liquidation
to go wrong
hoover
proven (success)
retailer
with hindsight

10b: Going global

Globalisation

acquisition
adaptation
to add value
business plan
to centralise
economies of scale
to expand
to export
franchise
globalisation
joint venture
know-how
licensing agreement/arrangement
local knowledge
ownership
pay-off
to retain (control)
returns
risk-free
takeover
target market
wholly-owned (subsidiary)
worldwide

General

exclusive(ly)
to exploit
high-margin (products)
mid-price (products)
retirement

	Written functions	Spoken functions
Giving information	Please note that ... I would like to inform you that ... I trust you will find the following points of interest.	Here's the information you wanted.
Asking for information	I would/should like to know ... Could you send me ...? I would be grateful if you could inform me ... I am writing to enquire about ...	I'd like to know ... Could you send me ...? Can you tell me ...?
Checking information	Please let me know asap. Could you let me know as soon as possible? Could you please confirm ...? I would be grateful if you could confirm ...	Let me know ... I need to know ... There are a few details I'd like to check. Sorry, I didn't get that. Could you say that again?
Reminding	Let me remind you that ... May I remind you that ...?	Remember that ... Don't forget that ...
Making requests	Please ... Please could you ...? Could you please ...? I would be grateful if you could ... ... are requested to ...	Can you ...? Please could you ...? Do you think you could ...? Would you mind -ing ...? I wonder if you could ...
Suggesting/Recommending	How about ...? What about ...? Perhaps we could ... We should ... I suggest ... I propose ... I would recommend ... It is suggested that ... It is proposed that ...	How about ...? What about ...? If we ..., we could/should ... (I think) we should ... Let's ... Why don't we ...? Perhaps we could ... Couldn't we ...?
Thanking	Thank you (very much) for ... I would like to thank you for ... I am very grateful for ... It was very kind of you to ...	Thanks for ... Thanks very much for ...

Answer key

Unit 1a: Teamwork (Self-study)

Ex ❶: 1 B   2 C   3 C   4 C
         5 A   6 B   7 B   8 A

Ex ❷: 2 When would suit you? / Did you have a day
            in mind?
         3 how about / what about
         4 When would suit you? / Did you have a time
            in mind?
         5 What about / How about
         6 I'm afraid I'm busy then. / I'm sorry but I can't
            make it then.

Ex ❸: *Suggested answers:*
         1 The courses are designed to develop team
            leadership skills.
         2 Is your team successful?
         3 I work in a multi-cultural team.
         4 We all contribute to the team.
         5 Communication needs to be improved in the team.
         6 Teams have to be managed well in order to be
            effective.

Ex ❹: 2 're launching
         3 isn't going
         4 'm beginning
         5 agree
         6 want
         7 Are you meeting
         8 don't have / haven't got
         9 do you think
        10 don't care
        11 've got / have

Unit 1b: Communication (Self-study)

Ex ❶: 1 tell   2 call   3 put back
         4 sensitive 5 raise   6 ask
         7 adapt   8 get

Ex ❷: ▯1 Good afternoon. Pace Systems. Can I help you?
         ▯2 Could I speak to Paul Kerridge, please?
         ▯3 I'm afraid he's in a meeting. Could I take a
            message?
         ▯4 Yes, please. I'm ringing about accommodation for
            his trip to Berlin. I've booked him a room at the
            Alsterhof Hotel for three nights from 22 August.
         ▯5 So that's the Alsterhof Hotel for three nights from
            22 August. Could you spell the name of the
            hotel for me, please?
         ▯6 Sure. That's A-L-S-T-E-R-H-O-F.
         ▯7 And could I ask who's calling, please?
         ▯8 It's Kerstin Meier from Althaus Press in Berlin.
         ▯9 OK, Ms Meier. I'll give Paul the message.

         ▯10 That's great. Thanks very much. Bye.
         ▯11 Thanks for calling. Bye.

Ex ❸: 1 S   confirming an appointment
         2 W
         3 W   changing an appointment
         4 S
         5 W   asking for confirmation
         6 S
         7 W   talking about availability
         8 S
         9 S   asking for permission
        10 W
        11 S   making an offer
        12 W

Ex ❹: 1 at   2 in   3 on   4 at   5 on
         6 at   7 on   8 in   9 at 10 on

Ex ❺: 2 You don't need to order them because I've **already**
            done it.
         3 The goods arrived **on Friday**.
         4 They haven't phoned the suppliers **yet**.
         5 I didn't have much experience **when I started**.
         6 We've been very busy **lately**.
         7 She's **just** gone to lunch but she'll be back in an
            hour.
         8 The company was founded by two brothers **20
            years ago**.

Ex ❻: 2 haven't been
         3 used
         4 did
         5 've tried
         6 have worked
         7 said
         8 told
         9 hasn't done

Unit 1: Exam practice

R4:   1 C   2 A   3 B   4 D   5 C
        6 D   7 B   8 A   9 C   10 C
       11 A   12 C   13 C   14 A   15 D

R5A: 1 WITH   2 ON
        3 A   4 CORRECT
        5 AGAINST

W1(i): *Suggested answer:*   (35 words)
        To: All staff
        From: Mr Port

        *I would like to inform you that as of 14.11.99, the new
        name for our company will be MasonGolding. Please
        note that from this time, only the new company name
        should be used.*

        Thank you.

W1(ii): *Suggested answer:* (33 words)

Jim

Could you please contact Team-Plus to book a team-building event for two days for eight of our sales staff?

I suggest the weekend of 24/25 November or the following weekend.

Thanks.
Alan

Unit 2a: Entertaining a client (Self-study)

Ex ❶: 1 with   2 on   3 on   4 to
5 at   6 for   7 in/by   8 for
9 until/till   10 from

Ex ❷: 2 How did the meeting go?
F Not bad, I suppose. We did make some progress.

3 What's your hotel like?
E Very comfortable, thanks.

4 How was the restaurant?
A Wonderful. And it had a great atmosphere.

5 What was your flight like?
H Fine, thanks. There were no delays this time.

6 Did you have any problems finding us?
C Not at all. I just followed your instructions.

7 Did you have a good journey?
I Fine, thanks. It only took a couple of hours.

8 What did you think of the place?
G I didn't really get a chance to look around.

9 When did you get here?
D Just a few minutes ago. Sorry I'm late.

Ex ❸: 1 satisfaction   2 located   3 comfortable
4 cleanliness   5 entertainment

Ex ❹: 3 Did you?   4 Do you?
5 Couldn't they?   6 Have you?
7 Aren't they?   8 Is she?

Ex ❺: 1 wasn't it?   2 isn't it?   3 hasn't it?
4 do you?   5 have you?   6 didn't it?
7 will you?   8 isn't there?

Unit 2b: Corporate hospitality (Self-study)

Ex ❶: *Suggested answers:*
1 I was delighted
2 We would like to invite you
3 I would be grateful if you could tell me
4 I do hope
5 I look forward to hearing from you

Ex ❷: 1 free   2 social   3 golden
4 poor   5 missed   6 valued

Ex ❸: 1 of   2 up   3 at   4 in   5 to

Ex ❹: 2 fact-finding mission   3 trade fair
4 sightseeing tour   5 shopping trip
6 sports event

Ex ❺: 1 meet   2 finalise   3 place
4 build   5 set

Ex ❻: 1 businesses   2 advice
3 is   4 information
5 is   6 much
7 a little   8 many
9 luggage   10 experience
11 knowledge   12 a little

Unit 2: Exam practice

R2: 1 G   2 H   3 A   4 D   5 E

R1: 1 A   2 B   3 D   4 B   5 C
6 A   7 C

Unit 3a: Ordering goods (Self-study)

Ex ❶: 2 Could you please confirm the date? / Could you confirm the date, please?
3 May I remind you that ...?
4 Further to your letter of ...
5 I would be very grateful if you could ...
6 Thank you for your fax concerning ...

Ex ❷: *Suggested answer:* (105 words)
Order no. BS/453

Dear Mr Jenkins
I am writing concerning the above order, which we placed with you on 23 March 1999. This order was for the following items:
- 300 short-length 'Scarlette' skirts
- 200 medium-length 'Suzanne' skirts.

I regret to inform you that due to restructuring changes within our organisation, we have been forced to make large-scale cuts to the contents of our forthcoming catalogue.

As a result, we have to cancel our order for the 200 'Suzanne' skirts.

I can confirm that the proposed delivery date of 22 August 1999 for the 'Scarlette' skirts is acceptable.

I apologise for any inconvenience this change to our order may cause you.

Yours sincerely

Ex ❸:

1 p i e **c** e s
2 q u **a** l i t y
3 s h o r **t** e n
4 c **a** n c e l
5 m a i **l** o r d e r
6 v e n d **o** r
7 l e n **g** t h
8 r e d **u** c e
9 b u y **e** r

Ex ❹: 1 recommended 2 finalise
3 delivery 4 measurements
5 suppliers 6 standardise

Ex ❺: 2 ● are you leaving ▼ 'm going to order
3 ● are you doing ▼ 'm going to relax
4 'm visiting
5 'll fax
6 ● are you taking / are you going to take
  ▼ 'll try

Unit 3b: Cash flow (Self-study)

Ex ❶: *Suggested answers:*
1 We can offer you a cash discount of 2%.
2 Some customers pay cash on delivery.
3 The cash price is 1% lower than the normal price.
4 We can pay in cash or give you a cheque.
5 Their cash flow situation is getting worse.
6 We can't pay until the end of the month because of a cash shortage.
7 He made a cash payment of $2,000 when he placed his order.
8 If his cash forecast is correct, we'll need to see the bank about a loan.

Ex ❷: 1 on 2 for 3 in 4 at
5 within 6 of 7 as

Ex ❸: 1 down payment
2 outstanding balance
3 30 days net
4 early settlement discount
5 penalty charges
6 cash on delivery

Ex ❹: 1 terms 2 supplies
3 labour 4 customer

Ex ❺: 1 don't / 'll 2 insisted on / 'd
3 might / look 4 increase / will
5 wouldn't / did 6 would / were

Unit 3: Exam practice

R2: 1 C 2 F 3 A 4 H 5 E

R5A: 1 CORRECT 2 IT 3 THE
4 CORRECT 5 BEEN

R5B: 1 FOR 2 AS 3 DEVELOPING
4 THE 5 EXPECTED

Unit 4a: Brand power (Self-study)

Ex ❶: *Suggested answers:*

to damage	power
own	**(a) brand**	stretching
major	loyalty

Ex ❷: 1 entered / targeted 2 growing
3 set up 4 boosted
5 saturated 6 diversify
7 target / enter / break into 8 enter / break into

Ex ❸:

Verb	Noun	Adjective
commit	commitment	committed
diversify	diversification	diversified
saturate	saturation	saturated
attract	attraction	attractive
rely (on)	reliability	reliable
strengthen	strength	strong
encourage	encouragement	encouraging
grow	growth	growing

Ex ❹: 1 with 2 into 3 up 4 with
5 to 6 for 7 with 8 to

Ex ❺: 2 loyalty scheme 3 supermarket chain
4 competitive advantage 5 own-label clothing

Ex ❻: ● Sven, how are the preparations going for the new product launch?
▼ They're going OK. **We're going to** launch the new product with a TV campaign in about three weeks.
● A TV campaign? **That'll / That's going to** cost a lot of money.
▼ Well, we think it's such an important product that **we're going to** spend half our advertising budget on it.
● Half the budget? What else **are you going to** do?
▼ Well, **we're going to** use a lot of point-of-sale advertising and do a mailshot next month.
● **Will it / is it going to** target only existing customers?
▼ At first, yes. But if the TV ads go well, then **we'll / we're going to** do a larger follow-up mailshot. **We'll** have to see what happens.

Ex ❼: 1 Customers are (more) likely to buy (more) products.
2 Diversification is set to continue in the future.
3 There are bound to be some problems.
4 I've no doubt it'll happen soon.

Unit 4b: Public relations (Self-study)

Ex ❶: 1 B 2 A 3 C 4 B
5 B 6 C 7 A 8 B

Ex ❷: *Suggested answers:*
1 A Choose and book the venue.
2 C Send invitations and monitor the replies.
3 A Prepare information packs and send them to the printers.
4 D Shortly before the launch, brief all staff involved.
5 F Check everything and finalise the details.
6 B Ensure all guests have access to the products.

Ex ❸: 1 brand 2 product
3 campaign 4 company
5 invitation 6 display

Ex ❹: 1 responsibility   2 awareness
          3 independent   4 availability
          5 reputable   6 dissatisfied
          7 advertisements   8 coverage

Ex ❺: 1 the   2 an   3 the   4 the
          5 the   6 Ø   7 Ø   8 the
          9 Ø   10 a

Unit 4: Exam practice

R1:   1 B   2 A   3 C   4 D   5 C
        6 A   7 B

R4:   1 C   2 A   3 D   4 B   5 A
        6 D   7 D   8 C   9 A   10 D
       11 B   12 C   13 A   14 A   15 C

Unit 5a: Relocation (Self-study)

Ex ❶: 1 costs   2 rates   3 tariffs
          4 overheads   5 savings   6 grants
          7 investment

Ex ❷: 1 assess   2 offers   3 arranges
          4 conclude   5 fulfils   6 compare
          7 recommend   8 is made / be made
          9 have been approached

Ex ❸: 2 Ireland has a high**ly** effi**cient** distribution network.
          3 Ireland offers compa**nies** financial incen**tives** to
             se**t** up busi**ness**.
          4 Ireland has a highly sophis**ticated** telephone
             net**work**.
          5 The cos**ts** of runni**ng** a compa**ny** are very
             attra**ctive**.

Ex ❹: 1 greater than
          2 more varied
          3 the most advanced
          4 the highest
          5 more spectacular than
          6 the most cosmopolitan
          7 even better
          8 less high than / not as high as
          9 even more quickly than
        10 the same as / the biggest

Unit 5b: New premises (Self-study)

Ex ❶: 1 impressive   2 fast-growing   3 easy
          4 numerous   5 immediate   6 wide
          7 major   8 available

Ex ❷: if you look right, you'll see ..., on the corner, walk to ...,
          turn left / right, cross over, take the first road on the
          right, keep going along ... until you come to ..., keep
          straight on till you reach, take the first right / left , on
          the left / right, you go down there, halfway along is ...,
          it's on the right, you can't miss it

Ex ❸: *Suggested answer:*   (40 words)
          *Go out of the station and turn right. Walk straight on
          past the theatre on your left, and then take the next
          right. Take the first road on the right after that. Go
          past the bakers and turn left. Then go through the
          square. We're the big white modern building on the
          right.*

Ex ❹: *Suggested answers:*
          1 I'd like to know about availability.
          2 And which floors are free at the moment?
          3 Can you tell me about car parking facilities?
          4 How far away are they exactly?
          5 Do you think you could put something in the post?

Ex ❺: *Suggested answers:*
          public transport, shops, bars, restaurants, goods lifts,
          underground car parking, reception, toilets,
          natural light, standby generator

Ex ❻: 1 tenant   2 appointment
          3 renovation   4 location
          5 premises   6 square metres
          7 property

Ex ❼: 1 excited
          2 confusing
          3 interested
          4 disappointed
          5 shocked
          6 fascinating

Unit 5: Exam practice

L1:   1 training course
       2 Managing People
       3 13(th) August / August 13(th)
       4 887762
       5 4.30 / four-thirty / 16.30
       6 Roughton
       7 Gatwick (airport)
       8 main offices / main reception
       9 Measuring Performance
     10 Conference Room
     11 cassette player
     12 £250 / 250 pounds

L2:   13 B   14 F   15 A   16 E   17 C
       18 B   19 G   20 F   21 E   22 C

L3:   23 A   24 C   25 A   26 B   27 A
       28 C   29 B   30 A

R5A: 1 CORRECT   2 UP   3 WITH
        4 CORRECT   5 AND

Unit 6a: Reporting results (Self-study)

Ex ❶: 1 rose   2 collapsed
          3 shooting up   4 peaked
          5 fall   6 recovery

Ex ②:

		¹d	i	v	i	d	e	n	d				
		i											
		s		²n							³t		
⁴p	r	e	t	a	x						u		
		o		t				⁵c	o	r	e		
		s			⁶a						n		
⁷a	c	q	u	i	s	i	t	i	o	n			
		l			s					v			
			⁸i	n	v	e	s	t	m	e	n	t	
					t					r			
					s								

Ex ③: 1 at   2 from / to
3 in   4 by / of

Ex ④: 2 The favourable exchange rate led to / meant an increase in profits.
3 Sales fell as a result of / due to bad weather in the summer.
4 Strong competition led to / meant a reduction in margins.
5 The share price collapsed as a result of / due to bad publicity.

Ex ⑤: 1 suddenly   2 substantial
3 steady   4 hard
5 marginally   6 dramatically

Unit 6b: Environmental report (Self-study)

Ex ①: *Suggested answers:*
performance, legislation, questionnaire, project, investment, regulations, impact, programmes, issues, improvements

1 project   2 legislation / regulations
3 impact   4 improvements / programmes
5 issues   6 performance

Ex ②: 2 comply with / fulfil (a legal obligation)
3 concentrate / focus (on a problem)
4 assess / evaluate (a proposal)
5 address / deal with (a complaint)
6 recognise / realise (a problem)

Ex ③: 1 consumption   2 subsidised
3 obligatory   4 compliance
5 threat   6 hazardous
7 spending

Ex ④: 1 B   2 C
3 B   4 A
5 B   6 C
7 C   8 C
9 A   10 B
11 A   12 B

Unit 6: Exam practice

R4: 1 B   2 A   3 D   4 C   5 A
6 D   7 A   8 D   9 B   10 C
11 A   12 D   13 C   14 B   15 B

R5A: 1 ONE   2 CORRECT   3 CORRECT
4 OUT   5 WHICH

W1(i): *Suggested answer:* (38 words)
To: All staff
From: Paul Blake

Please note that all paper used in the office will now be recycled. It should be placed in the green bin next to the photocopier for collection. All staff are asked for their full cooperation with this scheme.

W1(i): *Suggested answer:* (30 words)
To: All staff
From: Marie Santer

The computer system will be shut down all day on 15.12.99 to allow upgrading work to be carried out. Could you please prepare alternative work for this day?

Thank you.

Unit 7a: Health and safety (Self-study)

Ex ①: 1 arise   2 protect   3 lift
4 slipped   5 incidents   6 injured
7 hurt   8 precautions   9 required
10 personnel

Ex ②: 1 harmful   2 injury / injuries
3 obligation   4 findings   5 hazardous
6 safety   7 liability

Ex ③: 1 out / off   2 of   3 for   4 for
5 on   6 into   7 from   8 from

Ex ④: 1 needn't   2 could   3 Shall
4 can   5 must not   6 will
7 could   8 May   9 might
10 don't need to   11 should   12 could

Unit 7b: Rights at work (Self-study)

Ex ①: 1 deal with   2 draw up   3 put up with
4 meet   5 keep up with   6 prioritise

Ex ②: *Suggested answer:*
right, unfair dismissal, to rule (on / that), case, to be faced with legal action, to bring before a tribunal, to award damages, claims, to enforce, to breach an obligation, grievance

Ex ③: 1 grievance   2 stay   3 fault
4 observe   5 damage   6 complain
7 frequent   8 meet   9 disturbed
10 right

Ex ④: exaggeration, justification, abuse, ban, behaviour, negotiation, refusal, complaint

Ex ⑤: 1 C   2 E   3 A   4 D   5 B

Ex ⑥: B   He was dismissed.
         C   No action was taken against him.
         D   He was given an official written warning.

Ex ⑦: 2 was taken over   3 has just been told
         4 'll be offered   5 's offered   6 been told

Unit 7: Exam practice

R3: 1 G   2 C   3 A   4 F
      5 D   6 F   7 G   8 B

R5B: 1 BY   2 ALL   3 THIS / THE
       4 WHICH   5 PROVIDING

W1: **Suggested answer:**   (32 words)
      To: Head Office staff
      From: Susan Beck

      I would like to inform you that Ms Francesca Bianchi is
      the new Sales Manager at Head Office. Please give her
      a friendly welcome when she starts work next Monday.

      Thank you.

Unit 8a: Business expenses (Self-study)

Ex ①: **Suggested answers:**
      1 when was the trip exactly?
      2 what kind of business trip was it?
      3 how did you get to Paris?
      4 where did you stay?
      5 how many nights did you stay there?
      6 what was the name of the client you took to
         dinner?
      7 Could you spell that for me, please?

Ex ②: 2 random check
      3 small print
      4 line manager
      5 short notice

      1 line manager
      2 short notice
      3 random check
      4 false claim
      5 small print

Ex ③: to claim
      to incur
      to claim back
      to pay   **expenses**
      to handle
      to deduct

      to make
      to handle
      to process   **an expenses**
      to monitor   **claim**
      to submit

Ex ④:

Verb	Noun
supply	**supplier**
reimburse	**reimbursement**
claim	**claim**
authorise	**authorisation**
require	**requirement**
automate	**automation**

Ex ⑤: Dear Mr Rivers

      I enclose the expenses claim that (**that** can be
      omitted) you sent to me last week as it is incomplete.
      I need to know the names of the clients that (**that**
      can be omitted) you took for lunch and the name of
      the restaurant where you took them (or **which you
      took them to**). I also need to know the reason for the
      £25 **that / which** (**that / which** can be omitted) you
      put in the last column. Please also note that it is only
      line managers **who / that** can authorise expenses, not
      colleagues **who / that** work in your office.

Ex ⑥: 1 Mr Fuller is the client **who / whom / that / Ø** I took
         to lunch.
      2 Employees **who / that** travel on company business
         will be sent a form by e-mail each month.
      3 The new expenses claims system, **which** will be
         implemented next month, will cut costs
         considerably.
      4 I received the expenses claims form **which / that / Ø**
         you sent me last week.
      5 Those are the employees **whose** expenses we paid
         last week.

Unit 8b: Business travel (Self-study)

Ex ①: 2 baggage allowance   3 check-in desk
      4 scheduled flight   5 in-flight catering
      6 reclining seat   7 priority status

Ex ②:

- able	- ing	- ive
reasonable	annoying	exclusive
transferable	disappointing	competitive
bearable	reclining	selective
refundable	entertaining	

Ex ③: 1 H   2 B   3 E   4 A   5 I
      6 C   7 G   8 D   9 F

Ex ④: 1 for   2 on   3 for   4 for
      5 at   6 with   7 in / of   8 In

Ex ⑤: 1 survive   2 compete   3 transfer
      4 raise   5 undercut   6 fail

Ex ⑥: 2 I'd like to know when we take off.
      3 Can I just ask if this ticket is refundable?
      4 Could you tell me why there is a delay?
      5 Could you tell me if we get a meal on board?

Ex ❼: *Suggested answers:*

1 Could you tell me if there is any in-flight entertainment?
2 I'd like to know if you offer a frequent flyer programme.
3 Can I just ask where the business lounge is?
4 Could you tell me what time we leave?
5 I'd like to know if the seats are reclining?
6 Can you tell me where I can exchange money?

Unit 8: Exam practice

R4:

1 C	2 D	3 A
4 A	5 A	6 D
7 C	8 B	9 B
10 A	11 C	12 D
13 A	14 D	15 C

W2: *Suggested answer:* (113 words)

Dear Mr Chandler
Re: Order no. B13/4620

Thank you for your letter of 28 June. First of all, I would like to apologise for the unsatisfactory handling of your order.

Deliveries have unfortunately been delayed by several weeks due to the truckdrivers' strike. However, this dispute has now been settled and I am pleased to inform you that we can replace your two damaged desks next week.

As for the invoice, as an established customer you should indeed have received a 10 per cent discount. I enclose the amended invoice and trust that you will accept a further 2% discount for the inconvenience caused.

I would like to assure you that future orders will be dealt with reliably and efficiently.

Yours sincerely

Unit 9a: Flexible benefits (Self-study)

Ex ❶: *Suggested answers:*

childcare vouchers, additional cash, retail vouchers, (personal) accident insurance, travel insurance, pension, company car, health insurance, life assurance, medical insurance, company car

Ex ❷:

2 pension scheme   3 lump sum
4 bargaining power   5 payroll costs
6 annual leave   7 bulk discount
8 staff turnover

Ex ❸:

1 diversity   2 implementation
3 Maintenance   4 challenging
5 optional   6 recruitment
7 security   8 awareness

Ex ❹:

1 to   2 off
3 in   4 of
5 for   6 in
7 on   8 for

Ex ❺:

1	to put	2	providing
3	meeting	4	to select
5	to find	6	purchasing
7	make/to make	8	having
9	Choosing	10	dealing
11	to select	12	review
13	to suit		

Unit 9b: Staff appraisals (Self-study)

Ex ❶: *Suggested answers:*

1 She's co-ordinating the project and setting the group's objectives.
2 We're working towards unrealistic targets.
3 She'll really have to concentrate on meeting her objectives.
4 Did he achieve his target last month?
5 Could we please review my sales target for the current year?
6 We've set ourselves a range of objectives for the coming year.

Ex ❷:

1	ensure	2	praise	3	meet
4	evaluated	5	duties	6	promotion
7	update	8	policy		

Ex ❸:

2 well   3 successfully/well
4 frustration   5 develop

Ex ❹: *Suggested answer:* (37 words)

To: Lisa Bradley
From: Mary Parker

Re: Invoice No. 21692

Dear Mr Bradley

I apologise for the delay in paying the above invoice. This is due to a computer error in our Accounts Department. I can assure you that the invoice will be paid in full today.

Ex ❺:

+ (that)	+ infinitive	+object + infinitive	+ abou
say agree promise explain mention complain	promise agree	ask someone to ...	ask talk complai agree

2 She promised to send the report that day.
3 She complained about the amount of feedback she got.
4 She explained that the mistake had been due to a computer error.
5 She told him not to mention pay at the start of the appraisal.
6 She agreed to raise the price.
7 He asked me to look for a suitable venue.
8 He mentioned that there was a trade fair on the following week.

Unit 9: Exam practice

R2: 1 E 2 B 3 H 4 C 5 F

W2: *Suggested answer:* (120 words)
Dear Ms Garcia

I am writing to point out a few changes to the original itinerary for Wednesday 20 October. Firstly, your tour of the company will be slightly shorter than hour we originally planned. Secondly, please note that as the White Hart is full on Wednesday, lunch will be at the Swan Hotel. Carol Snape will, however, not be joining us due to a previous engagement.

It has been confirmed that Tom McAllister will show the new video about our new natural shampoo range at 16.00. As John Sallis has to leave early, Sue Smith will accompany you to the airport for your evening flight.

If you have any questions, please do not hesitate to contact me.

Yours sincerely

Unit 10a: Marketing disasters (Self-study)

Ex ❶: advertising, (advertising) campaign, (promotional) event, to organise an event, promotional gift, complimentary flight, to run / enter a competition, winner, first prize to, boost sales, publicity photos, (catchy) slogan

Ex ❷:
1 market
2 marketing
3 Marketing
4 market
5 market

Ex ❸:
2 undercut competitors
3 attract customers
4 withdraw a product
5 run a competition
6 avoid a mistake
7 win market share
1 run a competition
2 attract customers
3 boost sales
4 win market share
5 undercut competitors
6 avoid mistakes
7 withdraw a product

Ex ❹:
2 The confectionery company should have made the clues more difficult.
3 The petrol station chain shouldn't have held the promotion at the same time as the Twins Society Convention.
4 The petrol station chain could have postponed its promotion.
5 The building company should have anticipated the problems that arose.
6 The building company shouldn't have allowed flat-

owners to enter the competition.

Ex ❺:
2 The senior managers would have kept their jobs if the company hadn't lost so much money.
3 If customers had repaid the computer retailer earlier, it wouldn't have gone out of business.
4 If customers hadn't preferred the original flavour of Coke, the company wouldn't have had to relaunch it.

Unit 10b: Going global (Self-study)

Ex ❶:
2 know-how
3 joint venture
4 takeover
5 decision-making
6 team-building

Ex ❷:
2 long-term (plans)
3 worldwide (communication)
4 wholly-owned (subsidiary)
5 risk-free (venture)
6 high margin (products)

Ex ❸: *Suggested answers:*
1 Xtol has increased its share of the Russian market.
2 Marten has been priced out of its target market.
3 They lack knowledge of the local market.
4 The export market is reported to be steady.
5 Consumer confidence in the market is growing.

Ex ❹:
2 made an acquisition
3 a failure
4 complete ownership of
5 licensing agreement

Ex ❺:
2 have only managed
3 looks
4 spoke
5 thinks / thought
6 entering
7 is travelling / is going to travel
8 has been doing
9 have learnt
10 are going / have been going
11 to enter
12 will avoid
13 experienced

Ex ❻:
2 Their news **was** very encouraging.
3 It's the service **that** really matters.
4 I look forward to **hearing** from you in due course.
5 This type of problem is very **normal**.
6 We are very **interested** in your product range.
7 I didn't manage **to finish** all the work on time.
8 **Whose** offer did you finally decide to accept?
9 The report **is based** on the most recent figures.
10 The company is a lot bigger **than** it used to be.
11 Last year's sales figures have to be **checked**.
12 So the company's doing well, **is it?**
13 It's a lot **harder** to find clients than keep them.
14 She didn't give me **much** advice on what to do.

15 When I told him the problem, he **told** me that it
wasn't important.

Unit 10: Exam practice

L1:
1 Unit 5
2 Office Manager
3 photocopy paper
4 Thursday
5 Regional Manager
6 Competitive salary
7 current salary
8 26(th) April / April 26(th)
9 (Marie / Mrs / Madame) Delorme
10 Research Director
11 his / the company
12 Confirm flight

L2:
| 13 F | 14 E | 15 G | 16 A | 17 H |
| 18 D | 19 A | 20 B | 21 H | 22 C |

L3:
| 23 C | 24 C | 25 A | 26 C | 27 B |
| 28 B | 29 B | 30 A | | |

R5B:
| 1 ALSO | 2 ALL | 3 LEAST | 4 TO |
| 5 THE | | | |

Look it up

Do you want to learn more about the language and topics covered in *Pass Cambridge BEC 2*? The table below shows you how to find out more information using **Linguarama English Reference Guide 2** and the Internet.

		Language	Skills	Unit	Website
1a	Teamwork	Verbs + prepositions		35	www.coverdale.co.uk
1b	Communication		Telephoning	67-69	
	Self-study	Present tenses Past simple and present perfect		1-2 3, 6	
2a	Entertaining a client	Making conversation		53, 57	
2b	Corporate hospitality	Making invitations	Letter writing	55 85	www.FT.com
	Self-study	Countability		38, 40-41	
3a	Ordering goods		Letter writing Telephoning	85 67-69	
3b	Cash flow	Conditionals 1 & 2		15-16	www.toolkit.cch.com
	Self-study	Intentions and arrangements Conditionals 1 & 2		2, 10-11 15-16	
4a	Brand power				www.j-sainsbury.co.uk
4b	Public relations		Letter writing	85	www.skoda-auto.cz
	Self-study	Futures Articles		10-11, 61-62 39	
5a	Relocation	Comparatives & superlatives Similarity & difference	Report writing	30 58 87	www.idaireland.com
5b	New premises	Making suggestions	Letter writing	64 85	
	Self-study	Comparatives & superlatives		30	
6a	Reporting results	Describing trends	Report writing	60 87	
6b	Environmental report		Presentations Report writing	70-74 87	www.ici.com
	Self-study	Adjectives and adverbs Determiners		28-29 39-43	
7a	Health and safety	Expressing obligation		24-25	
7b	Rights at work	Passives		12	www.companydigest.co.uk
	Self-study	Modal verbs Passives		20-27 12	
8a	Business expenses				
8b	Business travel				
	Self-study	Relative pronouns Indirect questions		33 31	
9a	Flexible benefits				www.pwcglobal.com
9b	Staff appraisal				
	Self-study	Gerunds & infinitives Reporting speech		18-19 31	
10a	Marketing disasters	Expressing hindsight		17	
10b	Going global				www.hostmarriott.com
	Self-study	Conditional 3		17	